D0925869

GOD

THE MASTER MATHEMATICIAN

GOD: THE MASTER MATHEMATICIAN
© 2002 by Dr. N. W. Hutchings

Printed in the United States of America

Published by
Hearthstone Publishing, Ltd.
P.O. Box 815 ▪ Oklahoma City, OK 73101
405/948-1500 ▪ 888/891-3300 ▪ *hearthstone@coxinet.net*

ISBN 1-57558-106-X

GOD

THE MASTER MATHEMATICIAN

DR. N. W. HUTCHINGS

FIRST EDITION
June 2002

Table of Contents

Foreword 7

The Bible—The Master Math Book 9

God—The Master Designer 20

Why All the Fuss Over Bible Versions? 29

Thank God for Number One 37

Two Heads Are Better Than One? 44

Three Is a Crowd 49

Four Corners on a Round Earth 55

Why Five Fingers? 61

The Six Billionth Man (or Woman) 72

TGIS—Thank God It's Saturday 80

Eight—It Ain't Over 'Til It's Over 87

Nine Apples and Oranges 90

Ten—Enough Is Enough 92

Eleven—Here Comes the Judge 94

God Has No Baker's Dozen 97

Going to the Thirteenth Floor 100

Pick a Number 104

New Math Isn't New 114

Looking for Your Star 122

Numbers in Prophecy 139

Foreword

On December 2, 1804, Napoleon Bonaparte was crowned emperor of France. It was customary for the pope to anoint the new kings of Europe with Divine rights from God, which was known as the "Divine Right of Kings," or "the king could do no wrong."

The pope had traveled all the way from Rome to Paris to perform his high priestly duties in placing the crown on Napoleon's head. But the vote to make Napoleon emperor and begin a new royal dynasty in France was rather close. Also, there was hangover resentment against the Catholic Church from the French Revolution, plus the historical memories of the Catholic participation in the slaughter of the Waldensens and persecution of the Reformation clerics were still present. In consideration of all the political and religious nuances, Napoleon abruptly put the crown on his own head, and then crowned his wife, Josephine, queen of France. The height of egotism or simply political astuteness?

Likewise, it is customary for the author to have one of his peers, or superiors, to write the foreword or introduction to his book, or books. I seldom, if ever, ask someone else to help verify my own opinions and/or mistakes. As my Grandma Askew used to say: "Every tub should sit on its own bottom."

Why is a book on biblical numerics important, or even needed? In the Bible there are thousands of numbers. A number like seven or four may be used hundreds of times. Numbers in Scripture fall into many patterns and designs. Should we not at least investigate how and why the forty or more writers of the sixty-six books of the Bible living over a time span of sixteen hundred years maintained the same numerical patterns and designs?

It is our conclusion that only a Master Mathematician could have guided the writers of the books of the Bible to maintain the numerical designs and patterns. It is the same Master Mathematician who placed the sun, Earth, and the moon at the precise distances so that life on Earth would be possible. It is the same Master Mathematician who figured the exact percentages of gases in our atmosphere, and the proportions of our bodies to sustain and maintain life and reproduction. We conclude that such a study will show that only God, the Master Mathematician, can account for Earth, our solar system, and the universe.

I also want to let the reader know that I have borrowed from others in the more complicated sections of the book, but most of the presentations are mine.

The Bible—
The Master Math Book

We are living, we believe, in that generation spoken of in Daniel 12:4: "But thou, O Daniel, shut up the words, and seal the book, even to the time of the end: many shall run to and fro, and knowledge shall be increased."

It has been claimed that today knowledge is doubling every two and one-half years. In times past, there have been periods in which knowledge has increased in certain areas of human intelligence: music, literature, agriculture, mechanics, etc. But in the present generation, there has been an explosion of knowledge in every facet of the laws of science that govern the universe and man himself: medicine, agriculture, metallurgy, aerodynamics, astronomy, electronics, nuclear physics, geology, mechanics, plastics, and communications. At the base of the knowledge explosion in these latter years is man's development and application of the science of mathematics and, in particular, computer science. A computer is a mathematical machine developed to the degree that it can apply the laws of mathematical science to any given problem and situation. Without the computer, modern space exploration would not have been possible.

The word "mathematics" comes from the Greek *mathematikos,* or the Latin *mathematicus,* and means "to learn," "inclined to learn," or "memory." A computer is a sophisticated mathematical machine, but it is only as useful as its memory. If a computer loses its memory, it is of no use. It is the ultimate projection and application of the meaning of the word mathematics, coined by the Greeks almost three thousand years ago. The coming fifth-generation computers will be living entities that will program themselves, operate themselves, and talk in any language. All the information in all the computers of the world today can be stored in the space of a sugar cube in the new computer. Such a computer could become the fulfillment of the "image of the beast" prophesied in Revelation 13. All the world will marvel at such an apparition that will command everyone in the world to worship the Antichrist as God, and no man or woman will be able to work, buy, or sell unless they have an assigned number and code mark.

The first computer I remember coming in contact with was in early 1944 on New Caledonia, an island in the South Pacific. I was a radar operator for an antiaircraft battalion in World War II. We had just received a new radar unit, which to us at the time was a miracle.

This new unit would figure the elevation and azimuth for the guns, and it would even set the fuses where they would explode within thirty feet of an incoming Japanese bomber. The greatly improved effectiveness of our guns was made possible by a unit about the size of a secretary's desk on wheels attached to the back of the radar van. I was told this was a computer. These first clumsy, vacuum tube computers can today be replaced with one no bigger than a fifty-cent piece.

Today, computers control travel, communications, and family life. If every computer in the world would shut down, planes would not fly; there would be no electricity; there would be no water; banks and supermarkets could not open; etc. Yet, computers are simply super-advanced adding machines based on God's intricate numerical designs.

However, God is infinitely greater than any computer today or any that are on the drawing board, because He is the Master Mathematician of the universe. He is the author of all science, and by His laws of creation all things consist.

The base of all absolute mathematics is the fact that one plus one equals two. From the beginning in Genesis, we read on the first day of creation that God spoke, and there was light. On the next day of creation, God spoke and the firmament, or our atmosphere, appeared. We read in Genesis 1:8: "And God called the firmament Heaven. And the evening and the morning were the second day."

The first chapter of Genesis plainly informs us that one plus one equals two. On the next day, God made the dry land and plant life appear, and here we are told that two plus one equals three. In Genesis we discover division. God divided Adam into two parts, and from one came two. We are also told that man, through procreation, multiplied upon the face of the earth.

Through the chronology of mankind in Genesis we see the development of the numerical system to nearly one thousand. Methuselah lived to be nine hundred sixty-nine years of age before he died. And from the beginning of simple arithmetic in Genesis we discover progressively the development of mathematics until Revelation, where there is revealed a complicated system of numerics involving patterns of sevens, tens, and other numbers. In Revelation 9:16 we find the number 200 million.

The mathematical structure of our Bible proves beyond doubt that it was written by a Master Mathematician; it could not possibly have been written by mere human beings alone. This numerical pattern lies beneath the surface of the original Greek and Hebrew texts from which our King James Version came. We understand that there are no truly original texts, because as far as we know the original letters or parchments upon which John, Luke, Paul, and the other writers of the New Testament wrote, have not been found. Perhaps the closest writings in existence to the original texts are those of the Dead Sea Scrolls containing portions of the Old Testament, including the Book of Isaiah. But from the original Greek, Hebrew, and Aramaic, upon which the Majority Text is based, there is found a remarkable scientific, mathematical pattern that proves that God, by the Holy Spirit, preserved the purity and perfection of His Word, just as the Holy Spirit moved upon the writers of the Old and the New Testaments.

Just as the Bible establishes the basis of all absolute mathematics, it also establishes the rule for all theoretical mathematics: a straight line is the shortest distance between two points. It is from this theorem that all other theorems and postulates from which geometry, trigonometry, analytics, and other branches of theoretical math spring. Jesus said in Matthew 7:14, "strait is the gate [or opening], and narrow is the way [or line], which leadeth unto life, and few there be that find it."

Not only is the shortest distance between point "A" (earth) and point "B" (heaven) a straight line, unless you find point "C" (Jesus Christ), you will never make it.

There are many reasons why we accept the Bible as the inspired Word of God. The words of the human writers of the Bible, forty in all writing over a time span of approximately sixteen hundred years, claimed that they were writing the words that God gave them. We read in Second Timothy 3:16, "All scripture is given by inspiration of God."

Second Peter 1:21 states that the Bible was written by holy men of God as they were guided, or moved, by the Holy Spirit. We read also in Luke 1:70, ". . . he [the Lord God] spake by the mouth of his holy prophets."

There are hundreds of other verses of Scripture which aver that the Word of the Lord came to the prophets as they wrote. We know also that the Bible is the Word of God because it shows the reader the way, the line, or the road, and that way is Jesus Christ, declared from Genesis to Revelation. We also are provided indisputable evidence that the Bible is not just another human book, but in its intricate numerical pattern was a guiding influence that guided the pen of Moses just as it did the pen of John as he wrote Revelation.

Let us take, for example, the number seven, God's perfect number. From the first book in the Bible through the last, seven is the most dominant number. God rested on the seventh day, or the Sabbath. Egypt experienced seven years of plenty and seven years of famine. When the city of Jericho was captured, the people and seven priests who had seven trumpets marched around the city seven times. Every seventh year the land of the Israelites was not to be cultivated or planted. Solomon spent seven years building the Temple. After its completion, he held a feast for seven days. Naaman washed seven times in the river.

In Revelation, the last book of the Bible, seven is mentioned repeatedly: seven churches, seven lamp stands, seven seals, seven trumpets, seven vials, seven stars, seven spirits, etc. In Revelation alone it is used more than fifty times. These are just a few examples of the evident usage of seven through the Bible, which prove that it is an unusual book. Forty writers who lived over a period of sixteen hundred years would not have continued the pattern unless there was a central author. Within the Hebrew and Greek texts is an even more amazing pattern of sevens.

In the first verse of the Bible, Genesis 1:1, the number of Hebrew words is seven. The total Hebrew letters in these seven words is exactly twenty-eight, or four times seven. The first three words contain the subject and predicate of the sentence. Translated in English it says: "In the beginning God created."

The total letters in these first three Hebrew words is exactly fourteen, or two times seven. The last four Hebrew words contain two objects of the verb "created": "the heavens" and "the earth." The total number of letters in the first object is exactly seven. The three dominant words in this verse are "God" (the subject) and the objects "heaven" and "earth." The total number of letters in these three Hebrew words is exactly fourteen, or two times seven. The number of letters in the other four words of the verse is also fourteen —two times seven. This is just one of countless numerical examples in the Bible which mathematically prove that the Bible is a supernatural, God-breathed, God-given book.

From the first book in the Old Testament we go to the first book in the New Testament, Matthew. The first chapter contains the genealogy of Jesus Christ recorded in the first seventeen verses. Christ's genealogy here is

divided into two sections:
1. From Abraham to the time of the Babylonian captivity and
2. From the Babylonian captivity to the Lord's birth.

The first division is contained within verses one through eleven; the second division from verse twelve through seventeen. The number of Greek words used in the first eleven verses is exactly 49, or 7 x 7. Even though a Greek word may be used more than once, it is still counted only once. The number of Greek letters used in these 49 words is exactly 266, or 38 x 7. Of these 266 letters, the number of vowels is exactly 140, or 20 x 7. The number of consonants is 126, or 18 x 7.

Of these 49 different Greek words, those which begin with a vowel are 28, 4 x 7. The number which begin with a consonant is 21, or 3 x 7. Of the 49 Greek words, the number which are nouns is 42, or 6 x 7. Those not nouns are seven. Of the 42 nouns in the first eleven verses, the numbers, which are proper nouns is 35, or 5 x 7; the number which are common nouns is seven. The number of times the 35 proper names occur is 63, or 9 x 7. Of the 35 proper names in the first eleven verses, we find there are 63, or 9 x 7. The number of times the 28 male names (4 x 7) occur is exactly 56, or 8 x 7. In the first eleven verses, three women are mentioned—Tamar, Rahab, and Ruth. The number of Greek letters in these three names is 14, or 2 x 7.

Only one city is named, Babylon, but the number of

Greek letters in Babylon is seven. Of the 49 Greek words which appear in the first eleven verses, the number of words which occur more than once are exactly 35, or 5 x 7. The number of words that occur one time are 14, or 2 x 7.

There are also patterns of sevens in the second division of Christ's genealogy contained in verses twelve through seventeen. In the remaining eight verses of Matthew 1:18-25, there are 77 different Greek words in the text, 11 x 7. Of the 77 Greek words, the number of words spoken by the angel to Joseph are 28, 4 x 7.

The second chapter of Matthew contains the account of Jesus' childhood. The number of Greek words in chapter two are exactly 161, or 23 x 7. The number of Greek letters are exactly 896, or 128 x 7. There are several paragraphs, and each paragraph has numerical features of its own. For example, the number of Greek words in the first six verses, 56, divides perfectly by seven (8 x 7).

From Matthew we go to the Gospel of Mark. The first eight verses of chapter one record the ministry of John the Baptist. The number of Greek words are exactly 77, or 11 x 7. Of these 77 words, the number which begin with consonants is 35, or 5 x 7; the number John used in his preaching is 21, or 3 x 7. In the account of Christ's baptism, the number of Greek words used in the text is 35, 5 x 7.

Going on to the second chapter of Mark, we find the calling of Matthew in verses thirteen through seventeen. The Greek words in these five verses are exactly 49, or

7 x 7. Of these, the number spoken by the Lord are 14, 2 x 7, while the number spoken by the scribes is exactly seven.

In Mark 4:3–20, Jesus relates the parable of the sower. In this parable the number of Greek words is exactly 49—7 x 7. In Mark 13:5–37, Jesus prophesied of future events and His coming again. The number of Greek words in the Olivet Discourse in Mark is 203—29 x 7. Mark 16:9–20 records the events after Christ's resurrection. The Greek words in these twelve verses are 98, 14 x 7. Of these 98 words, there are 553 Greek letters used, or 79 x 7. The number of words spoken by the Lord in addressing His disciples are 42, or 6 x 7.

These are just a few of the passages which prove that the entire Bible is one book with one author—God, the Master Mathematician. But God is not just the Master of math; He is the Creator and Ruler of the Universe. Inasmuch as every scripture is God-breathed, we can believe the words of Jesus Christ, Who declared that He and His Father are One, as recorded in John 3:16: "For God so loved the world, that he gave his only begotten Son, that whosoever believeth in him should not perish, but have everlasting life."

As we get into the study of specific numerical designs in the Bible, we will discover that four is the number of the world (four directions, four winds, four oceans, etc.). We read in Galatians 4:4: "But when the fulness of the time was come, God sent forth his Son, made of a woman, made under the law."

There was an exact date, a number on the calendar for Jesus to be born—four thousand years after the creation of Adam (*Ussher's Chronology*). There is also an exact date for Jesus to return. Jesus said that only God knows the date He will come back. But the unsaved do not have to wait for some date in the future to receive Jesus Christ as Savior. They do not have to wait until next year, next month, next week, or even tomorrow.

> . . . I have heard thee in a time accepted, and in the day of salvation have I succoured thee: behold, now is the accepted time; behold, now is the day of salvation.
>
> —Second Corinthians 6:2

God—The Master Designer

As we noted in the first chapter, the basis of the science of mathematics is established in the Bible from Genesis to Revelation. The numerical structure of the Bible proves that it was not just a book of many authors written over hundreds of years, but as Scripture declares, there was one Author, God Himself, Who gave each writer the words to write as led by the Holy Spirit.

One of the most interesting studies relating to the mathematical structure of the Scriptures is that of numeric values. In Hebrew and Greek, every letter, word, sentence, and passage has a definite numeric value or sum. The Hebrews and Greeks did not use figures such as 1, 2, 3, or 4 to count numeric value. Rather, they used the letters of their alphabet. For example, if a Hebrew or a Greek wanted to write "1," he would write the first letter of the alphabet. If he wanted to write "2," he would write down the second letter of the alphabet, etc. Each letter in the Hebrew and Greek alphabet stands for a certain number; every letter is a number, as well as a letter.

Since each letter has a numeric value, each word,

phrase, or sentence has a sum total. The numeric sum of a word is obtained by adding the values of the various letters in that particular word, phrase, or sentence. The most important word in the Bible is the name of Jesus. In Greek, Jesus is spelled "I-E-S-O-U-S." "I" is 10, "E" is 8, "S" is 200, "O" is 70, "U" is 400, and "S" is 200. If we add these numbers, we find the numerical value of "Jesus" is 888. Every number in the Bible is important or else it would not be there, because every word, even every jot and tittle in the original text, was God-breathed. When we turn to Revelation, we find that Satan's number, or the number of Antichrist, is 666. Thus, we realize there must also be significance to the number of Jesus, 888.

In our first study, we considered the mathematical pattern of the first verse in the Bible. Let us now consider the three important nouns in Genesis 1:1, the subject and dual predicates: God, heaven, and earth. The numeric values of these three words are 86, 395, and 296 respectively. When we add these three numbers we get a sum of exactly 777, or 111 x 7. If another word had been used or another value assigned any letter in any of the three words, the mathematical pattern would have been broken. The numeric value of the Hebrew verb "created" in the first verse is exactly 203, or 29 x 7.

In our first study we also discussed the mathematical pattern in Matthew 1:1–17 which gives the genealogy of Jesus. In addition, the numeric sum of the different Greek words used in these verses is 42,364 or

6,052 x 7. Again, if another word had been used in these seventeen verses, the pattern would have been broken.

We also mentioned that the words in the account of Christ's birth in Matthew 1:18–25 is exactly 77, but it is even more amazing that the numeric value of these 77 words is exactly 51,247 or 7,321 x 7. Again, if even one Greek letter had been different in any of these 77 words, the pattern would have been broken. We mentioned that the angel used 28 different words, 4 x 7, when speaking to Joseph. The sum total of the value of these 28 words is exactly 21,042 or 3,006 x 7. We also referred to chapter two of Matthew, which gives the account of Christ's childhood. The number of different words used is 161 or 23 x 7, and the numeric sum of these words is exactly 123,529 or 17,647 x 7.

The man's name that appears more than any other in the Old Testament is David. His name is found in the Old Testament exactly 763 times or 109 x 7. Moses' name occurs in the Bible 847 times, or 121 x 7, and Jeremiah is mentioned 147 times in seven Old Testament books, or 21 x 7.

There are only two possible ways in which these intricate and complicated numerical patterns could have occurred. They could have been the result of an almost inconceivable coincidence, or they could have been the result of a determined design followed and calculated by the writers themselves. This would have been almost impossible; firstly, because the writers lived in different centuries, and secondly, each would have needed access to one of our most modern computers in order to calculate and carry out the numerical pattern. The obvious answer is to believe what the writers of the Old and New Testament books said they wrote as God instructed them by inspiration and command of the Holy Spirit. These thousands of complicated mathematical patterns could only have been planned and calculated by a Master Mathematician, God Himself.

There are doubtless some skeptics who might yet claim that these numerical patterns occurred by accident. Let us consider the odds against these occurring by some monstrous fate of chance. Consider the odds against a pattern of seven occurring in a verse of scripture like Genesis 1:1, or Matthew 1:1–17. Only one number in seven is a multiple of 7; the other six numbers have just as good a chance to appear as seven. The chance of 7 appearing in a list of seven numbers by accident is, of course, one in 7. According to the law of chance, for any two numbers to be multiples of seven accidentally is one in 7 x 7, or one chance in 49. For four numbers to be multiples of seven is one chance in 2,401. In the case of 10 factors, the odds would be one in 282,475,249. The odds in 24 factors being multiples of seven would be one in 199,581,231,380,536,414,401. Many brief Bible passages have as many as 100 or more numeric features in the structure of their text. The odds against this happening would tax the memory of even a fifth-generation computer to calculate.

Suppose, for example, you were carrying a bag which

contained 24 oranges when suddenly, it came apart and the oranges fell on the kitchen floor. When the oranges stopped rolling they were arranged in four perfect rows with six in each row, each orange being exactly opposite the other and an equal distance apart. The odds against this occurring are just as astronomical as finding 24 numerical factors in a passage of Scripture divisible by 7.

For mere human beings like Matthew, Mark, Luke, or John to have purposely determined to have designed and written a single chapter to conform to an established mathematical pattern would have taken a lifetime. Dr. D. B. Turney related how he attempted to construct a passage that would show some numeric features, and he concluded:

> I gave numeric values to the English alphabet, and tried to prepare a passage which would adhere to the numerics, and make every section a multiple of seven, and present all the other features of biblical arithmography, without letting the meaning of the passage descend to nonsense. After working thereon for days, I could get no satisfaction. Yet this feature is accomplished in every one of the thousands of Bible paragraphs without the slightest visible effort.

Not only are the phenomenal designs confined to the text of single Bible passages, but widely separated portions of the Bible are woven into intricate and perfect patterns. Special words, which are scattered through many different books of the Bible form amazing chain designs that are filled with numerical features. The numeric designs in the structure of the Bible writers' names, for instance, extend through the entire Scriptures. The discovery of such word chains requires careful searching in all parts of the 66 books of the Bible.

The double design of seven in the name "Moses," for example, could not have been planned and carried out by the Bible writers themselves. Again, we point out that the writers did not live at the same time—they lived many years apart over a span of sixteen hundred years, and only a few knew each other, or even met. These were also men of different backgrounds, and many had little or no schooling. How would the Apostle John, who lived fifteen hundred years after Moses, have known to mention Moses only once in Revelation to complete the perfect numerical design of the name of Moses throughout the Bible? That example is only one of a complicated chain design which extends through the entire Bible. Each word is linked and connected in one continuous pattern. All the separate and intricate mathematical designs within individual passages are linked together to form one grand design. One of the most amazing truths about this is that the New Testament is linked with the Old Testament. This should prove to the Jews that the New Testament is a fulfillment of the Old Testament, and that Jesus Christ is, in deed and in truth, the Messiah promised by Moses, Daniel, and the other Old Testament prophets.

The minds of the cleverest men who have ever lived would not be capable of devising such sublime mathematical problems. No human could possibly have devised such a means of binding the whole of God's Word together. Only the author, God Himself, the Supreme Intellect of the universe, could have done it. The number of words found in Matthew, not found in any of the other twenty-six books of the New Testament, reveal mathematical designs so profound that they amaze us. How did Matthew know to use the right number of certain words to complete the pattern? In order for Matthew to have accomplished this, it would have been necessary to have had all the other books before him as he wrote, as well as the prison epistles of Paul not yet written, and the three epistles of John and the book of Revelation.

The Bible is different from all other books in the world including the Koran, the holy book of the Moslems, and the religious writs of the Hindus and Buddhists. The infallible numeric structure of the Bible proves that it is the only book written by an intellect superior to that of man. It is evident that the Bible is not the work of many minds, but the work of One Mind. The designs furnish clear proof that the whole Bible has but One Author, and each book of both the Old and New Testaments was written by the same Mind Who planned everything before the world's foundation. He is God, the Creator, Who said in Genesis 1:3: ". . . Let there be light: and there was light."

In fact, every candid, logically-minded individual is compelled to admit to himself, if not openly, that the intelligence which planned and designed the Bible was Superhuman, Divine. That One Designer was Supernatural, the Master Designer, the Master Mathematician. The Bible proves itself in Second Timothy 3:16–17: "All scripture is given by inspiration of God, and is profitable for doctrine, for reproof, for correction, for instruction in righteousness: That the man of God may be perfect, throughly furnished unto all good works."

The evidence and fact are such that no critic can successfully face them. Facing them means unconditional surrender to the inevitable and foolproof system which can stand any amount of honest testing. No living person has yet attempted to dispute this convincing array; the best anyone can do is to ignore them.

Robert Ingersoll, a noted infidel of the past, was continually asking for a miracle from the Bible. He taunted his Christian debater to take the Bible and perform a supernatural act beyond human capability and understanding. In the very Word and context of our Bible are hundreds of miracles.

In geometry, the two angles at the base of an isosceles triangle are proved to be equal by cold, unimpassioned mathematical reasoning, about which there can be no dispute. Divine inspiration of the Bible is proved with all the evidence of mathematical precision. The overwhelming evidence shatters all arguments of atheists and agnostics. The Word, backed by indisputable scientific and mathematical design, states in no uncertain terms that God, the Creator of the Universe, sent Jesus Christ, born of the Holy Spirit in the womb of a virgin, to die for the sins of every man and woman in the world. All who accept this truth, believe it, and receive Jesus Christ as personal Savior and Lord, are born again to eternal life. Anyone can receive Jesus Christ as Savior wherever they are at this very moment. God has proven to everyone who reads this message that He means what He says. It is up to the readers to prove to God that they mean what they say. Now is the accepted time to make the most important decision of your life.

Why All the Fuss Over Bible Versions?

Those ecclesiastics addicted to the newer version of the Bible based on the Westcott and Hort texts are usually quick to condemn any study of biblical numerics as nothing short of pure hocus pocus. The reason is that newer versions are generally based on dynamic equivalency rather than literal equivalency; therefore, if the translators or revisers generally capture the meaning of the Hebrew and Greek texts, then that is good enough. Also, some of the newer versions leave out entire verses, sentences, or paragraphs. Generalizing, omitting, or adding, destroys the perfection of God's Word. Numerical patterns become weakened or nonexistent.

Michael Hoggard, author of *By Divine Order: Scripture Numerics and Bible Prophecy,* stated in his book:

> It cannot, at least for now, be proven that every single number in the Bible has any great significance. Many are, however, finding out more and more of the mysteries of the Scriptures in these last days. It is the

opinion of this author that to omit or otherwise change any of the numbers found in the Scriptures is a mistake that should be avoided at all costs. The problem that many of the modern translations have is that they have, in many cases, changed the numbers, usually by converting weights and measures into current standards, or by completely omitting a number, replacing it with an invented paraphrase. Allow me to give one example of this. In John 6, the story of the feeding of the 5,000 is given. In the Authorized Version, verses 5–7 are recorded as follows:

"When Jesus then lifted up his eyes, and saw a great company come unto him, he saith unto Philip, Whence shall we buy bread, that these may eat? And this he said to prove him: for he himself knew what he would do. Phillip answered him, Two hundred pennyworth of bread is not sufficient for them, that every one of them may take a little."

Notice the difference between this and its corresponding verses from the New International Version (NIV).

"When Jesus looked up and saw a great crowd coming toward him, he said to Philip, 'Where shall we buy bread for these people to eat?' He asked this only to test him, for he already had in mind what he was going to do. Philip answered him, 'Eight months' wages' would not buy enough bread for each one to have a bit!"

Not only has the number been omitted, but a

paraphrased interpretation has taken its place. The phrase "eight months' wages" is not contained in any of the Greek texts. I am curious as to how a regular student of the Bible is supposed to know that two hundred pennyworth is the amount that a person would be expected to earn in eight months' time. Is this idea or equation located in the Bible anywhere? No. I do not doubt that someone has done some digging into ancient history and discovered something, somewhere, that told him that a man earned two hundred pennyworth in eight month's time. Isn't this a case of relying on man's knowledge and not God's? Those who translated this passage obviously made the assumption that God really intended to tell John to write it down as eight month's wages, but never got around to it, until the NIV was published. Please, don't do God any favors!

As you can probably tell, I am a stickler for leaving the Bible the way it is. You will see why I feel this way as you read this book. Although I may not have a flawless apologetic for the KJV, I am content with leaving it intact, not making any changes to any portions of it, and letting God supply the interpretation He wants.

The Contemporary English Version (CEV) has Philip saying, "Don't you know that it would take almost a year's wages just to buy only a little bread for each of these people."

Here we see "dynamic equivalency" at work. In addition to the two hundred pennyworth, the reviser has to get his own two cents worth into the text. The New American Standard Version (NASV) has Philip mentioning that two hundred denari would be needed. A pennyworth is a small English coin and a denari is a small Roman coin. If the purpose of the newer versions is to simplify the language, why go backward to Latin?

Another interesting numerical manipulation is Revelation 14:20 where we read in the King James Version that at the battle of Armageddon blood will be up to the bridles of horses for sixteen hundred furlongs. The NIV has the blood running for sixteen hundred stadia. The Contemporary English Version has the blood turning into a river for about two hundred miles and almost deep enough to cover a horse. The NASV simply has the blood running for two hundred miles at the horses' bridles.

According to *Webster's Dictionary*, "stadia" is a surveyor's instrument, and the unit of length is "stadium," in Greece between 607 feet and 738 English feet. In Rome a stadium was 609.95 feet. The *Davis Dictionary of the Bible* gives a furlong, based on the Greek Text, from 600 feet to 604 feet. The dictionary gives the length of a furlong at 220 yards. If a furlong is 220 yards, then 1,600 furlongs would be 200 miles. However, the Greek 1,600 stadiums would be only 172 miles.

Ed Vallowe in his book *Biblical Mathematics,* explained the reason for keeping numbers in scriptures in their unchanging orders and values:

1. All the simple numbers from 1 to 40 have a spiritual meaning attached to them. Above 40 only a certain group of numbers will have a special spiritual meaning applied to them.

2. Numbers compounded of these numbers, e.g., by doubling or trebling, generally carry the same spiritual meaning only intensified.

3. Numbers compounded by adding two simple numbers together usually carry the two meanings of such numbers, expressed together, bringing out a deeper spiritual truth.

4. Where a compound number is divisible by several factors, it will usually be found that its spiritual truth, if any, is hidden behind its simplest factors, that is, those which are incapable of further division.

5. The first use of a number in Scripture almost invariably gives the clue to its spiritual meaning.

6. A spiritual truth does not appear to be evidenced in respect of every place where a number appears.

7. Numbers are used to convey spiritual truths in at least three ways:

    a. By the actual use of a number.

    b. By the number of times a special word or phrase is used by the Holy Spirit.

    c. By the gematria of numerical value of a word or phrase.

E. W. Bullinger began his book *Number In Scripture* with the following introduction:

DESIGN SHOWN IN THE WORKS OF GOD

"Who hath measured the waters in the hollow of his hand, and meted out heaven with the span, and comprehended the dust of the earth in a measure, and weighed the mountains in scales, and the hills in a balance?" (Isa. xl. 12).

"The works of the LORD are great, sought out of all them that have pleasure therein" (Ps. cxi. 2).

There can be neither works nor words without number. We can understand how man can act and speak without design or significance, but we cannot imagine that the great and infinite Creator and Redeemer could either work or speak without both His words and His works being absolutely perfect in every particular.

"As for God, his WAY is perfect" (Ps. xviii. 30).

"The law of the LORD is perfect" (Ps. xix. 7).

They are both perfect in power, perfect in holiness and righteousness, perfect in design, perfect in execution, perfect in their object and end, and, may we not say, perfect in *number*.

"The LORD is righteous in all his ways, and holy in all his works" (Ps. cxlv. 17).

All His works were (and are) done, and all His words were spoken and written in the right way, at the right time, in the right order, and in the right number.

"He telleth the number of the stars" (Ps. cxlvii. 4).

"That bringeth out their host by number" (Isa. xl. 26).

"He weigheth the waters by measure" (Job xxviii. 25).

Bullinger's book on biblical numerics is the study source for most books on this subject, including this one.

But what difference does it make if the Battle of Armageddon is two hundred miles or sixteen hundred furlongs, if the distance is the same? The problem is with the interruption of the symbolic, numerical design. According to the composition of the armies that will fight at Armageddon, they will be provided the by king of the east, the king of the west, the king of the north, and the king of the south. They will come from the four directions of the world. Four is the number of the world. Ten times four is forty, the number of testing. Israel was tested in the wilderness for forty years; Jesus was tested of the Devil forty days, etc. Forty times forty is sixteen hundred, and God will bring all nations against Jerusalem. As Israel perished in the wilderness, God will destroy the armies of the world at Armageddon.

We are not so naive as some to contend that the King James Version was the work of the Holy Ghost and inspired men just as the writers of the original manuscripts. However, we do believe that God was with those men who, in a critical time of human history, came up with a translation that has been used to win hundreds of millions to a saving faith in Jesus Christ and change the world.

God admonishes us not to change one word, delete one word, or add one word to His preserved Word. If we are not to change one jot or one tittle, by what authority do men take liberties in changing numbers? The King James Bible is proven to be God honored in that it was the Bible used in spreading the gospel around the world from 1611 to our present century. In numerical design, why tamper with something that is already perfect?

Thank God for Number One

In the previous chapter we discussed evidence relating to the preservation of the Word of God in English through the King James Version of 1611. In this chapter we will discuss in detail how the mathematical pattern interwoven in the Hebrew and Greek texts has been carried on in the King James Version, proving that the Holy Spirit not only gave the Word of God to the prophets, but that He watched over and protected it as the Scriptures were copied and handed down through various scribes and Christian translators as they copied from succeeding manuscripts and passed them on to church leaders down through the centuries. For example, the Book of Isaiah in our King James Bible is the same as the English translation of the Book of Isaiah in the Dead Sea Scrolls copied by the Essenes.

A Look at the Whole Book

The Bible has 1,189 chapters, 31,175 verses, and 810,697 words. It is divided into two parts: the Old and the New Testaments. The first section has 39 books; the second section contains 27 books. In order to remember this numerically, the following has been worked out:

1. Old Testament. Old = three letters; Testament = nine letters; three and nine placed beside each other gives us thirty-nine books in the Old Testament.
2. New Testament. New = three letters; Testament = nine letters. Multiply three times nine to equal twenty-seven books in the New Testament.

Thirty-nine books in the Old Testament and twenty-seven in the New is a total of sixty-six books. The only book that bears "66" is Isaiah, having sixty-six chapters. Isaiah is a little Bible within the Bible.

1. The first chapter of Isaiah says: "Hear, O **heavens**, and give ear, O **earth** . . ." (Isa. 1:2). The first book of the Bible says: "In the beginning God created the **heaven** and the **earth**" (Gen. 1:1).
2. The last chapter of Isaiah says: "For as the **new heavens** and the **new earth**, which I will make, shall remain before me, saith the LORD . . ." (Isa. 66:22). The sixty-sixth and last book of the Bible says, "And I saw a **new heaven** and a **new earth** . . ." (Rev. 21:1).
3. Isaiah 40:3 says: **"The voice of him that crieth in the wilderness, Prepare** ye the way of the LORD, make straight in the desert a highway for our God." The fortieth book of the Bible, Matthew, 3:3 says: "For this is he that was spoken of by the prophet Esaias, saying, The voice of one crying in the wilder-

ness, Prepare ye the way of the Lord, make his paths straight."

Was this an accident?

The middle of the Bible is Psalm 118:8 which reads: "It is better to trust in the LORD than to put confidence in man."

With fourteen words, the two middle words are "the LORD." "The LORD" is in the middle of the King James Bible, "God" is in the beginning verse (Gen. 1:1), and "our Lord Jesus Christ" is at the end (Rev. 22:21).

United on Number One

There is no dispute among Bible-believing scholars about the meaning of number ONE. It very plainly means UNITY.

1. When God created Eve, He said that the man would "... leave his father and his mother, and shall cleave unto his wife: and they shall be ONE flesh" (Gen. 2:24). This is the UNION of man and woman in marriage.

2. "Hear, O Israel: The LORD our God is ONE LORD" (Deut. 6:4). Thus we have the UNION of the Divine nature. There are three in the Trinity, "... and these three are ONE" (1 John 5:7).

3. The UNION of the Lord Jesus Christ with His Father is seen in John 10:30: "I and my Father are ONE."

4. In Ephesians 4, Paul gives us the reason why born-again believers are to endeavor: ". . . to keep the UNITY of the Spirit in the bond of peace. There is ONE body, and ONE Spirit . . . ONE hope . . . ONE Lord, ONE faith, ONE baptism, ONE God and Father . . ." (Eph. 4:3–6).

5. In one man, Adam, all are condemned to death. In the one man, Christ Jesus, all will live forever. Those who remain in the condemnation of the first Adam will die eternally (1 Cor. 15).

6. One is the number of beginnings. The mathematician begins counting from one, and he or she can count forever and never run out of numbers to count.

7. God knows and considers each person individually as one man or one woman. Jesus wept for one man, Lazarus. Jesus Christ died for each individual man or woman, "whosoever believeth in him" (John 3:16). Each person as individuals, one man or one woman, will either be saved or lost. The saved will be rewarded individually: "every man shall receive his own reward according to his own labour" (1 Cor. 3:8). The lost will be judged individually: "and they were judged every man" (Rev. 20:13).

Thank God for the number one, for without it there would never have been the first day, the first light, the first dawn, the first man, or the first and only Savior, the ONE mediator between God and man.

On the first day of creation God performed a great

miracle. He created light: "In the beginning God created the heaven and the earth" (Gen. 1:1). As time started that first day, ". . . God said, Let there be light" (Gen. 1:3). Before God created any living thing He created light, because without light, no physical living thing could survive.

Has the reader ever thought how exceedingly complicated light is? The *American Heritage Dictionary* defines light as "electromagnetic radiation." The main source of light is our sun. Other stars within our galaxy, and planets within our solar system, afford minimal direct light or reflected light. Earth-based light can originate from burning flammable materials or electrical lighting systems, but without light from the sun, our planet would be a frozen ball void of all living things.

There are several theories as to what light is: the emission theory; the wave theory; the electromagnetic theory; the electron theory. Space does not permit an explanation of these several theories. There is a relationship between light and electricity. Both travel at an approximate speed of one hundred eighty-six thousand miles per second. The question is not why light travels this fast, but rather why it cannot travel faster.

By the nuclear generating process of fusion (not fission), hydrogen on the sun is converted to heat which in turn converts to light. Less than one percent of the light generated by the sun hits the earth, and it requires approximately eight minutes for a ray of light to travel from the sun to the earth. Albert Einstein proved that light has substance, or mass, and is subject to gravity. Perhaps this is why light has a fixed speed, else it might damage living things.

Light travels through a cold space approximately ninety-two million miles from the sun to Earth through temperatures of one hundred degrees below zero and more without losing its precious cargo of heat, yet when it strikes our earth, the heat is released. Wasn't God intelligent to think up such an ingenious way of heating our planet? It is unthinkable that this could occur by accident. Have you ever thought about thanking God for providing all this heat and light service without sending you a bill?

Light contains every color we see, and it resonates from forty-two hundred Angstrom wavelengths for violet, to seventy-two hundred Angstrom wavelengths for red. One Angstrom unit equals one ten-millionth of a millimeter. God created light so there would be life, and Jesus said that He was the light of this world.

It is clearly prophesied in the Bible that our sun will run down. It will no longer be able to generate light, but then, we won't need the sun. In the New Heaven and New Earth God will provide a new source of light: "And there shall be no night there; and they need no candle, neither light of the sun; for the Lord God giveth them light: and they shall reign for ever and ever" (Rev. 22:5).

The Lord calculated the exact speed of light so that we could see, the earth be warmed, and plants would grow. God also varied the speed of light rays so we could enjoy the individual, brilliant colors within light. Then, He must have determined the exact amount of hydrogen needed to make the sun so it would fulfill its mission until His plan and purpose for the First Heaven and the First Earth was completed. God is indeed the Master Mathematician.

Two Heads Are Better Than One?

Two Is Division

Take one apple and cut it in two, and of course, you have two parts. Even on the first day of creation God brought light into the void of darkness; thus, there were two elements. God divided the light from the darkness. There are two parts of the day—day and night.

We read that on the fourth day of creation God made two great lights—the sun and the moon, and on the second day of creation God divided the waters and placed the atmosphere in between. "And God said, Let there be a firmament in the midst of the waters, and let it divide the waters from the waters. . . . And the evening and the morning were the second day" (Gen. 1:6,8).

Three times Moses stressed that God placed part of the waters on earth above the firmament and part below the firmament. It is evident from the context that the firmament is the atmosphere which surrounds the Earth. It is thought by many scientists who accept the Genesis account of creation that before the Great Flood there was a large water vapor canopy above the Earth, possibly in the form of ice. This would have diffused light from the sun evenly over all the Earth resulting in a hothouse even-temperature effect. It is commonly reported that tree stumps and frozen animals, including the mammoth, are found today near the North Pole.

Moses also mentioned that there was no rain. The ground was watered by a thick fog or a "mist" (Gen. 2:6). This condition substantiates the water canopy, hothouse effect. Also, this condition, along with virgin soil, would have resulted in a plant explosion in the fifteen hundred years before the Flood, which would have made possible the sustaining of huge life forms like the dinosaur. A major catastrophe had to have occurred in order for all the vegetation and animals to have been buried in the ground and converted to fossil fuels like coal, oil, and gas. The Garden of Eden, according to the biblical location, would have been in the area of present Kuwait. It is no coincidence that Kuwait has more oil than any other place of comparable size. Those geologists who espouse the evolutionary theory contend this process of converting vegetable and animal matter to fossil fuels took millions of years, but the evidence in coal fields suggests the deposits occurred suddenly; thus, the conversion processes could have taken only decades, not ages.

The chemical composition of our present atmosphere at ground level is seventy-eight percent nitrogen; twenty-one percent oxygen; and one percent carbon dioxide and other gases. Some scientists who accept the Genesis account of creation believe that before the Flood the atmosphere contained a greater percentage of oxygen, and this would at least partially account for people living to be several hundred years old. In any event, the atmospheric composition had to have just the right balance of nitrogen, oxygen, and carbon dioxide to sustain both plant and animal life, so God must have known what He was doing to have put just the right amount of these gases in our air.

Animals need oxygen; plants need nitrogen and carbon dioxide. There are more plants than animals so the proration of gases in the atmosphere were mixed in the exact needed ratio. This also demonstrates beyond intelligent dispute that life was neither created, nor exists, by random chaotic chance. There must be a Supreme Designer who is not only a Master Mathematician, but also a Master Chemist.

Two Is the Number of Choice

God did not create beings, neither man nor angels, as robots. Adam and Eve were created as free moral individuals. They were given two choices: the Tree of Life or the Tree of Knowledge of Good and Evil. Men and women today also have choices:

1. The way of Cain (works), or the way of Abel (faith) (Jude 11; Eph. 2:8–9).
2. The God of this world (Satan); or Jesus Christ, Lord

of Creation (2 Cor. 4:4; 2 Tim. 2:10).

3. Heaven or Hell (Col. 1:5; Matt. 10:28).

4. The broad way, or the narrow way (Matt. 7:14).

It is the choice that men and women make between one of two options that not only determine their lives on this earth, but where they will live eternally.

Two Is the Number of Witness

"At the mouth of two witnesses, or three witnesses, shall he that is worthy of death be put to death; but at the mouth of one witness he shall not be put to death" (Deut. 17:6).

"One witness shall not rise up against a man for any iniquity, or for any sin, in any sin that he sinneth: at the mouth of two witnesses, or at the mouth of three witnesses, shall the matter be established" (Deut. 19:15).

The number two is the most important number in any nation's judicial system. A person accused of any wrong, including capital punishment, is not to be condemned without two witnesses who accuse him or her. While modern crime detection practices like fingerprints and DNA may serve as evidence in contemporary courts, the number two still stands as a principle of justice that no person be convicted of a crime without conclusive evidence.

Two Becomes One

God took a rib out of Adam and made Eve because He

determined that it was not good for man to be alone. A preacher's joke is that after that, Eve always counted Adam's ribs every day.

As we have noted, one of the properties of "two" is division. In Adam and Eve it might be concluded that two heads were better than one, but in their fall into sin in the Garden of Eden, this axiom may be debated.

In the taking of a rib from Adam, the Hebrew text indicates that the Lord took more than a rib from Adam. The personality of Adam was divided, but when Eve and Adam were joined together again in the marriage union, they became one flesh again. When a husband and wife are married in the will of God and dedicated to the principles of marriage as ordained by God, they become one in will and deed. When we see one we think of the other. Neither a man nor a woman can really be complete without a mate, and God's blessing upon their union.

Two is also the number of promise. God told the first two people that as husband and wife, they were to be fruitful and multiply. So God is not only the author of division, He is also the author of multiplication. He is indeed the Master Mathematician.

Three Is a Crowd

Jesus said: "For where two or three are gathered together in my name, there am I in the midst of them" (Matt. 18:20).

Perhaps this scripture was motivation for someone to first parrot the axiom, two is company but three is a crowd. As we presented in the previous chapter, God made the woman from Adam's rib. The two came together as one again and established the first home. After their first child, Cain, was born, there were three. This was the first family. The family is the base of every culture, society, and nation. The family is the brick that holds the entire structure together. If the roof leaks, it can be fixed. If the windows break, they can be replaced. If the bricks crumble, the entire home is lost.

Marriage, therefore, is ordained of God, but today it seems that at least fifty percent of the marriages crumble in divorce, and we witness a decaying, crumbling nation. I always tell others that I have a marriage made in heaven, because I like to fish and my wife likes to clean fish.

The Three Identities of God

Most numbers in scripture have primary and secondary meanings. God being first, and from the beginning takes primary precedence: "Go ye therefore, and teach all nations, baptizing them in the name of the Father, and of the Son, and of the Holy Ghost" (Matt. 28:19). "For there are three that bear record in heaven, the Father, the Word, and the Holy Ghost: and these three are one" (1 John 5:7). "The grace of the Lord Jesus Christ, and the love of God, and the communion of the Holy Ghost, be with you all. Amen" (2 Cor. 13:14).

God manifests Himself to men and angels in three ways, or personalities: Father, Son, and Holy Spirit. It is evident even in the first chapter of Genesis that the universe was the will of the Father; the Son created (Eph. 3:9); and the Holy Spirit brought life upon the creation (Rom. 8:9–11).

Three Identities of Man

Man was made in the image of God; therefore, man is a tri-part being (and of course when we say man we mean both sexes): "And the very God of peace sanctify you wholly; and I pray God your whole *spirit* and *soul* and *body* be preserved blameless unto the coming of our Lord Jesus Christ" (1 Thess. 5:23).

We find difficulty in trying to understand not only the Trinity of God, but also the trinity of man. The spirit in man motivates or wills; the soul is the personality.

We find in Scripture that the soul may be glad, sad,

and mad, etc. There is a continual battle in the spirit, the soul, and the flesh. Paul called this struggle the war of our members. If a man is accused of a crime, the defense cannot argue that the person is just mean spirited, or that he is just naturally an angry person, or that he has a good heart and soul, but that his flesh is weak. The law cannot just put the flesh, soul, or spirit in jail and let the other two members go free.

The three persons of the Godhead are truth, righteousness, and in one accord. The three entities of man are in continual warfare and sinful. ". . . There is none that doeth good, no, not one" (Rom. 3:12). This is why Jesus Christ had to die that the sinner be delivered from the penalty for sin.

The three noted apostates of the Bible are Cain, Balaam, and Cor'e (Jude 11).

The three temptations of man are: lust of the flesh, lust of the eyes, and the pride of life (1 John 2:16).

Men fight against the world, the flesh, and the Devil.

The Number Three In Jesus' First Advent
Jesus said in Luke 13:32: "Behold, I cast out devils, and I do cures today and tomorrow, and the third day I shall be perfected".

Jesus lay in the tomb three days and three nights. The Gospel entails the death, burial, and resurrection of Jesus. Jesus raised three from the dead: the widow's son, Jarius's daughter, and Lazarus. His three closest apostles were Peter, James and John.

DR. NOAH HUTCHINGS

The Third Day of Creation

"And God said, Let the earth bring forth grass, the herb yielding seed, and the fruit tree yielding fruit after his kind, whose seed is in itself, upon the earth: and it was so. . . . And the evening and the morning were the third day" (Gen. 1:11, 13).

In God's creative work on the third day, Moses emphasized twice that all plants were to reproduce only their own type. Chemists, biologists, or microbiologists may analyze an acorn and determine the exact amount of minerals, carbohydrates, proteins, acids, etc., in it; however, no scientist has been able to put all these compound elements together and make an acorn that would produce an oak tree. Scientists have continually attempted every experiment possible to put all the elements within living things together and bring forth life, but they have not produced even a one-celled amoeba. Only life begets life, and Jesus Christ, who created all things, declared, "I am the way, the truth, and the life" (John 14:6).

There is no evidence that a chemical or electrical accident ever produced even the most minute form of life.

The Creator locked the reproduction of plants, family within family, type within type, species within species, in the basic units of life—chromosomes. Each living cell in plants or animals contains a certain number and pattern of chromosomes. Grain species of plants normally have twenty to forty-two chromosomes in each cell structure. Some plants have as many as four hundred chromosomes. Chromosomes contain DNA, thousands of genes, which determine the future growth of the plant: leaves, roots, bark, fruit, limbs, wood, variety, etc. There is no evidence that mutations or natural selection changes the genetic patterns. Hybrids can be developed within related varieties, but hybrids do not reproduce. Also, genetically engineered plants, through recombinant DNA, revert back to their original basic identity. Every plant continues to reproduce after its own kind just as recorded in Genesis.

What would the world be like without plants? There would be no bread; no fruit; no vegetables; no grass—therefore no meat; no birds; no primates; no flowers, etc. Much of our medicine comes from plants. Plants also breathe in carbon dioxide and breathe out oxygen, and this process is so complicated biologists have difficulty in explaining it. Plants also take the minerals and vitamins we need from the soil, and when we eat the vegetables, we maintain a healthy and proper diet. Isn't it wonderful that God, on the third day of creation, created plants?

There are millions of different kinds of plant life. There are over two hundred fifty thousand kinds of flowering plants alone. Each plant has its own complicated cycle of pollination. In China, we once had a guide, a young chemist, who continually proposed the theory of evolution to our tour members. During one evolution speech, I pitched him an acorn and asked if he could tell me the ratio of proteins, acids, and carbohydrates in this acorn. He answered, "No problem." Then I asked him why he could not put all these ingredients together and make an acorn that would produce an oak tree. He had no answer. As the poet said, "Only God can make a tree." Mathematically, there must be the right percentage of sun, air, and soil for plants to grow. To figure all these percentages out for millions of plant varieties indeed required a Master Mathematician.

If there were only one blade of grass in the universe, it would be an unfathomable miracle.

Four Corners
on a Round Earth

It is to be understood that a book could be written on each number from one to twelve as they are presented in their various numerical patterns in Scripture. However, even if a publisher could be found to publish a five thousand-page book, few readers would buy it, much less read it. To inform in an interesting way is one thing; to drown the readers in a subject is quite another. I detest writing a dull book; therefore, let us see if we can find something interesting about the biblical number four: "And after these things I saw four angels standing on the four corners of the earth, holding the four winds of the earth, that the wind should not blow on the earth, nor on the sea, nor on any tree" (Rev. 7:1).

It is easy to determine that in the Bible, four is the number of the world. The world and its systems include the forces and characteristics of the earth, and all living things on the earth. But what about the four corners of the round earth?

I remember a NASA picture that was carried by the

news media in the 1970s shortly after satellites began orbiting the earth. This particular picture taken from space did show four bulging points on the earth an equal distance from each other. The caption accompanying the picture claimed that earth really did have four corners. However, the Greek word for corner in Revelation 7:1 is *gonia,* which means angle, not exactly a corner.

Two thousand years before Columbus set out to prove the earth was round, the prophet Isaiah wrote: "To whom then will ye liken God? or what likeness will ye compare unto him? . . . It is he that sitteth upon the CIRCLE of the earth . . ." (Isa. 40:18,22).

King David also wrote: "The heavens declare the glory of God; and the firmament sheweth his handywork. . . . His going forth is from the end of the heaven, and his *circuit* unto the ends of it . . ." (Ps. 19:1,6).

There are no scientific errors in the Bible; it is astrophysically and mathematically perfect, because the Author is the Master Mathematician, the Sustainer of every scientific law.

Moses recorded that on the fourth day of creation God made the "stars," and a "greater light" for the day and a "lesser light" for the night (Gen. 1:14–19). On the first day God created light, and some explain the creation of the sun and the moon on the fourth day as being hidden from the Earth because of a dense fog. However, God did not need the sun and the moon for light. There was light before the sun, and there will be light after there is no sun (Rev. 22:5).

The sun is a medium-sized star with a diameter of eight hundred sixty-five thousand, four hundred miles, approximately one hundred times that of earth. The mass of the sun is three hundred thirty-three thousand times that of earth. A two hundred-pound person on earth would weigh six thousand pounds on the sun. The earth makes a circuit around the sun every three hundred sixty-five and one-quarter days, while the sun is traveling seven hundred thousand miles per hour around the center of our galaxy, taking its nine planets along for the ride. The sun is a thermonuclear energy-creating instrument, converting hydrogen to helium to heat and light. The earth actually receives less than one-billionth of the energy produced by the sun.

The moon is a satellite of earth with a diameter of approximately one-fourth that of earth, and with mass and gravity only a fraction of our planet. However, the gravitational pull is sufficient to make ocean tides from three to five feet. The distance of the moon from the earth ranges from two hundred thirty-eight thousand miles to two hundred twenty-one thousand miles. Also, orbits of planets around the sun are not perfect circles. Some, like Velikovsky and Patton, have concluded that the orbits of the moon and the planets were once even more elongated, and this evidence would explain the biblical catastrophes as well as the geology of Earth, when in the past circuits of moon, Mars, or Venus, brought them nearer to Earth.

The September 29, 1999, edition of *USA Today* reported a NASA discovery of a nova-collapsed star in the supernova Crab nebula with a diameter of only twelve miles, revolving thirty-three times a second, where a teaspoon of matter weighs billions of tons. The light from the power generated by this nova is sufficient to illuminate the entire Crab nebula, one light year across. All these mighty revelations in the heavens being shown to this generation are to reveal the reality, the glory, and the awesome power of the Creator (Ps. 19:1).

Since the fourth day of creation our sun has been providing light and energy for our solar system, but according to the plan and purpose of God, this solar mission will end. For the past two thousand years sunspots and solar flares have been observed as increasing. These could be signs of an impending nova. The nova of a star occurs when the nuclear generator starts a meltdown process similar to what happens occasionally in nuclear plants on Earth, except billions of times greater. The star becomes brighter and hotter for a period of seven to fourteen days, the atoms are stripped of their shells, and the entire mass is compressed into a small ball only a few miles across, where gravity may become so intense that even light may not escape.

According to the prophetic Word, during the Great Tribulation the sun will become seven times brighter, and then become dark (Isa. 30:26; Rev. 16:8–9; Joel 2:31; Matt. 24:29). Also, at the same time, the moon, which reflects the light of the sun, will become hot, and then become dark also. Nevertheless, regardless of what happens to our sun, moon, or Earth, all who have been saved by faith in Jesus Christ will shine as the stars forever (Dan. 12:3).

The number four in all its worldly associations from Genesis to Revelation is to again prove that mere men could not have written the Bible.

1. There are four earthly elements: earth, air, fire, and water; and four oceans.
2. There are four earthly directions: east, west, north, and south (Isa. 43:5–6).
3. There are four world empires: Babylon, Medo-Persia, Greece, and Rome (Dan. 2).
4. There are four seasons of the year: spring, summer, fall, and winter.
5. There are four angelic watchers over God's creation on earth (Rev. 4:6–11).
6. Jesus Christ was born four thousand years after Adam, according to biblical chronology.
7. The birth, ministry, death, and resurrection are presented in the four gospels: Matthew, Mark, Luke, and John.
8. Jesus rose from the tomb at the beginning of the fourth day.
9. Four parts of the animal kingdom are: man, beasts, fowl, and fish.
10. Man's enemy has four names: Devil, Satan, Old Serpent, and Dragon (Rev. 20:2).
11. The sheet on which all living things had been made

clean was on a sheet with four corners (Acts 10:11).
12. In the Tribulation, four angels will destroy one-third of men in the world (Rev. 9:14–15). The New Jerusalem will be four square.

Four is mentioned approximately four hundred times in the Bible, and we could present four hundred examples of how this number is woven in the sixty-six books to prove that only a Master Mathematician Who also controlled the writings of the prophets could have accomplished such a marvelous composition.

On the fourth day when God made the sun, the moon, and the planets of our solar system, mathematical perfection was involved. Had the sun been made a little smaller or the earth placed a little farther away from the sun, life on earth, as we know it, could not have existed. Or, if the sun were made a little larger, or the earth placed a little closer to the sun, excessive temperatures would have prevented advanced forms of life. It took an exact mathematical equation to determine the orbit of the earth for life to be possible.

Reason dictates that a very special Creator with a very special plan made this world. Praise God, He is coming back to destroy those who are trying to destroy it (Rev. 11:18).

Why Five Fingers?

At times when I am typing on my 1952 Royal type-writer, I look at my hands and wonder why I have only five fingers on one hand. I can still click along at something like eighty words a minute, but if I had ten fingers, perhaps I could type twice as fast. But then, I would have to get a new typewriter specially made, and my brain would have to work twice as fast in composing sentence construction and thought.

Then, I wonder why I have five toes on each foot, but only two ears, two eyes and two legs. But even more puzzling is why I have only one nose and one mouth. Who decided or who constructed this strange design of our bodies?

Upon further analysis, I concluded that with four fingers and a thumb I can do just about anything I want to do—type, fish, play golf, use a fork or even chopsticks, and grasp a hot cup of McDonald's coffee. Also, two legs are nice. It would not be too enjoyable hopping around on one leg. Two ears located at the highest point of my body helps me to locate the direction of sound, so when my wife screams for me to take out the garbage, I run to the kitchen instead of grabbing my golf bag and heading for the golf course. My two eyes, also located near the top of my head, help me apply the mathematics of trigonometry for triangulation to judge distance. In the beginning God took pity on me so that I would not overrun stoplights and get a lot of traffic tickets.

It is true that primates have five digital extensions on their hands, but they do not have an opposable thumb. Primates' hands are fine for picking bananas off trees, but not very good for typing, writing, or flying an airplane. And while primates have two legs, their pelvis construction prevents walking in a ninety-degree upright position. There are also serious brain differences between primates and human beings. Yet, if evolutionists want to say the only difference between primates and man is the thumb, let them speak for themselves, but leave me out.

As far as one nose is concerned, I can smell as much as I want to with one, and I put too much already in the one mouth I have. Besides, think what your dental bills would be if you had two mouths.

King David wrote in Psalm 139:13–18:

For thou hast possessed my reins: thou hast covered me in my mother's womb. I will praise thee; for I am fearfully and wonderfully made: marvelous are thy works; and that my soul knoweth right well. My substance was not hid from thee, when I was made in secret, and curiously wrought in the lowest parts of the earth. Thine eyes did see my substance, yet being unperfect; and in thy book all my members were written, which in continuance were fashioned, when as yet there was none of them. How precious also are thy thoughts unto me, O God! How great is the sum of them! If I should count them, they are more in number than the sand: when I awake, I am still with thee.

David presented truths about genetics three thousand years ago that have only been discovered in the last fifty years. At the instant the male sperm unites with the female egg, the numerical construction and size of every body part is predetermined through three million genes in forty-six chromosomes.

My point in the preceding dissertation is to prove that God has perfectly planned our physical being—mathematically, numerically, and proportionally. Of course, I wish He would have made me look a little more like Clark Gable, and athletically a little more like Michael Jordan. However, He has given me seventy-nine good years, so why complain. And, overall, in considering how God made the six billion human beings alive on earth today, we have to marvel—what a Master Mathematician.

According to the book of Job, our days are numbered, our steps are numbered, and Jesus said even the hairs on our head are numbered. And indeed they are, because the number is predetermined in our DNA. God also predetermined the numerical ratio of all living things. It has been proposed that if the fly had no enemy, within a few months flies would stack up across the world ten feet high.

Moses wrote of God's creations on the fifth day: "And God created great whales, and every living creature that moveth, which the waters brought forth abundantly, after their kind, and every winged fowl after his kind: and God saw that it was good" (Gen. 1:21).

In the Scriptures we find that God cursed the ground three times for man's own good. After each curse the environment, along with plant and animal life, was affected. However, there is no mention of God cursing the seas and oceans; therefore, all varieties of marine life would still be in evidence today. A fossil of a fish which marine biologists named *coelacanth* was found, and because there was no evidence of such a fish in existence today, evolutionists considered it a valuable missing link from 410 million years ago, becoming extinct seventy-five million years ago. However, beginning in 1938, fishermen from Madagascar to Indonesia reported catching the fish. Some natives in East Africa depend upon this fish as a major food source.

Before the flood there were over three hundred different kinds of dinosaurs, some weighing up to one hundred thousand pounds. It is obvious that changing ecology after the flood could not support such animals. Some varieties of whales may weigh up to two hundred thousand pounds, but the sea ecology has changed very little.

The creation account stresses that the sea was to bring forth "abundant" life, and there are thousands of life forms in the sea with extremely complicated reproductive methods that can only be explained by special creation.

At one time there were birds much larger than the ostrich. These monster birds weighed several hundred pounds, but they also became extinct. Some smaller fowls became extinct because of changing environmental conditions or over-hunting. Most bird species have survived because they adapted to the environment. Different environments provide survival conditions for specific species of living things, not evolution of specific species.

That God created both fowl and marine life on the same day is especially interesting, because both forms of these living things needed to be specially equipped to survive in a changing world. Evolution cannot explain how a salmon can travel thousands of miles out into the ocean, and in four or five years find the exact mountain stream where it hatched from an egg. Or who can explain how migratory fowls can fly thousands of miles from polar regions to warm climates, and then back again in the spring? Or, why a monarch butterfly will fly from Canada to Mexico to survive the winter? Or, why bees with brains not much larger than a grain of salt can work together to perform the most complicated engineering tasks? Life itself is not only a miracle; the sustaining of life in challenging environments is equally a miracle that evidences the continuing shepherding of a benevolent Creator.

In view of the curse of sin upon the creation, we can understand why the whole creation is groaning, waiting for its restoration to its pristine estate before sin entered. This can only happen when Jesus Christ, by whom all things were created, returns (Rom. 8).

Getting back to our basic subject, from Genesis to Revelation God inspired the human recorders to put thousands upon thousands of numbers in the Bible— almost everything is numbered—added, divided, subtracted, counted in every detail. Why? These numbers are there to help you and I understand that only God could have authored the Scriptures.

In looking at our hands once more, why the number five? In the Bible, numbers not only represent mathematical values, but also letters in the original Greek and Hebrew manuscripts. But even more, numbers represent principles and God's very nature. I agree with Bullinger, Hoggard, and Vallowe in their books on Bible numerics, in that the number five represents God's grace to man, or the unearned favor from our Creator.

E. W. Bullinger, in his book *Number in Scripture* (pg. 135), said of grace:

> Grace means *favour*. But what kind of favour? For favour is of many kinds. Favour shown to the *miserable* we call mercy; favour shown to the *poor* we call pity; favour shown to the *suffering* we call compas-

sion; favour shown to the *obstinate* we call patience;
but favour shown to the *unworthy* we call GRACE!
This is favour indeed; favour which is truly Divine in
its source and in its character.

If my *Strong's Exhaustive Concordance* is correct, and my
counting is correct, in the King James Version "grace" is
found thirty-eight times in the Old Testament and one
hundred twenty-eight times in the New Testament. In
my Bible, the thirty-nine Books of the Old Testament
comprise seven hundred eighty-six pages; the twenty-
seven books of the New Testament comprise two hundred thirty-one pages. It should also be noted that in
the Book of Revelation, grace is found only twice—once
in the first chapter and once in the last chapter (Rev.
1:4; 22:21). This is just another indication that the seven
years of the coming Tribulation Period revert back to
the administration and dispensation of the Law, and the
Church is not found in the Tribulation—mid, post or
pre-wrath.

In the Old Testament under the law of both conscience and statute, God granted His grace individually.
The first illustration of His granting pardoning and for-
giving grace is in Genesis 6:5–8:

And God saw that the wickedness of man was great
in the earth, and that every imagination of the
thoughts of his heart was only evil continually. And
it repented the LORD that he had made man on the

earth, and it grieved him at his heart. And the LORD said, I will destroy man whom I have created from the face of the earth; both man, and beast, and the creeping thing, and the fowls of the air; for it repenteth me that I have made them. But Noah found grace in the eyes of the LORD.

The Scripture does not say anything about Ham, Shem, Japheth, or their wives, or Noah's wife finding grace with God—only Noah. Michael Hoggard, in *By Divine Order*, brings out the association of the number five with Noah finding grace with God:

1. Noah's name is first mentioned in the fifth chapter in the Bible;
2. His name is mentioned the fifth time when God grants him grace;
3. Noah was five hundred years old (100 x 5) after the flood;
4. The waters were on the earth one hundred fifty days (30 x 5), or five months;
5. Noah (Noe) is referenced five times in the Gospels.

It is believed by some that God took Adam's fifth rib to make Eve, because four others mentioned in the Bible suffered a deadly wound under the fifth rib (2 Sam. 2:23; 3:27; 4:6; 20:10).

Jesus' Name in the King James Version has five letters, and in Isaiah 9:6 He is given five titles: Wonderful,

Counselor, The Mighty God, The Everlasting Father, and The Prince of Peace. Christ is found five hundred fifty-five times in the New Testament—the first verse (Matt. 1:1) and the last verse (Rev. 22:21). He is indeed the Alpha and Omega, the Beginning and the End.

Jesus fulfilled the penalty of the Law for all who receive Him as their Savior. He offered Himself to complete the five offerings the Law demanded:

The Peace Offering;
The Sin Offering;
The Trespass Offering;
The Burnt Offering; and
The First Fruit Offering.

Jesus fed five thousand with five loaves of bread (Mark 8:19). Jesus was seen above five hundred brethren after He arose from the grave (1 Cor. 15:6). Paul was beaten with forty stripes save one, five times for preaching the gospel of grace. The last figure given of the Jews who believed that Jesus was their Messiah is "about five thousand" (Act 4:4).

There are five letters in grace, and we read in John 1:17 that ". . . grace and truth came by Jesus Christ."

But we also read in John 1:11–12, "He came unto his own [Israel], and his own [Israel] received him not. But as many as received him, to them gave he power to become the sons of God, even to them that believe on his name."

Peter and John continued to offer the Kingdom to Israel if the people would repent of killing their Messiah, and cry out to God to send Him back (Acts 3:11–21). There would have been no Gentile Church age.

When your doctor listens to your heart, he will place his stethoscope over your fifth rib, because that is the rib directly over your heart. Soldiers were trained to aim the spear at a spot between the fifth and sixth rib. It is probable that this would have been the rib where the side of Jesus would have been pierced on the cross. Not only would His heart have been pierced, but also the fifth rib would have signified that indeed God's grace had passed to all men through the sacrifice of His Only Begotten Son.

Inasmuch as the fifth rib is the only one of the twelve ribs directly over the heart, it is probably the rib that God would have taken from man to make the first woman.

Just considering the number five, from Genesis 1:1 to Acts 4:4, the number five is referenced some three hundred times. Most of these numbers are in association with God's promise of the coming Redeemer. But between Acts 4:4 and Revelation 9:1, five is referenced only five times. Numbering is a Kingdom promise identification. The gospel of grace is to believers the fulfillment of God's pardon through Jesus Christ our Lord. We who had no covenant, no Law, no animal sacrifices, no feast days, no Sabbath, no Temple, so undeserving, have been saved by God's love in sending His only Son to die in our place.

The next time the reader looks at his or her hand with five fingers, think of Ephesians 2:8–10, "For by grace are ye saved through faith; and that not of yourselves: it is the gift of God: Not of works, lest any man should boast. For we are his workmanship, created in Christ Jesus unto good works, which God hath before ordained that we should walk in them."

The Six Billionth Man
(or Woman)

In the year 2000, world census reports indicate that the earth's human population reached six billion. We do not know the identity of the person who tipped the counter at six billion, and it probably does not matter anyway.

We do know according to the biblical creation that man, along with other forms of land-dwelling animal life, was created on the sixth day. "And God said, Let the earth bring forth the living creature after his kind, cattle, and creeping thing, and beast of the earth after his kind: and it was so" (Gen. 1:24).

On the sixth day of creation God created the thousands of different members of the animal kingdom apart from the plant kingdom. "Animals" means living things which are animated, or can move about. The animal kingdom is divided into two parts: cold-blooded animals and warm-blooded animals. These two divisions can then be divided again into many families and species.

All animals reproduce according to a predetermined genetic blueprint that cannot be altered; thus, every animal reproduces its own kind. A mouse and an elephant may have the same number of chromosomes in every cell, yet it is obvious that a mouse and an elephant cannot reproduce a mouphant. Within the same animal family, a hybrid may result, like the mule, but mules cannot reproduce any offspring. Evolutionists cannot prove that one animal ever evolved into another animal.

Dr. Francis Crick received a Nobel Prize in science work in genetics. He concluded that chromosomes, DNA, and the double helix—units of life involved in reproduction—were so miraculous that they could not have been developed by evolution. Dr. Crick could not acknowledge a special Creator; therefore, he concluded a civilization from another galaxy brought life to Earth. Of course, this is ridiculous; but even if true, Dr. Crick could not explain how such life could have developed in another solar system.

It is thought by many scientists who accept the biblical record of creation that dinosaurs died in the flood, or did not survive the post-flood era; however, some sub-dinosaur types, like the alligator and Komodo dragon, have survived even though other animal species have not survived. Los Angeles was built over the La Brea tar pits. In these tar pits are the bones of millions of animals; many are extinct, like mastodons, mammoths, giant sloths, giant bears, saber-toothed tigers, etc. Also in the tar pits are the bones of camels, giraffes, and African lions. If this latter group evolved, then they would have evolved at the same time on two continents separated by thousands of miles of water, which would be unthinkable. But can you imagine camels, giraffes, and African lions in California? Southern California, Arizona, and Nevada at one time were areas covered by rivers and lakes. As the environment changed, animal life was pressed closer to the ocean, and subsequently to the tar pits, the only liquid available in the summer months. This change occurred, we believe, during the four hundred years after the flood. Geologists and paleontologists agree that these animals died in the tar pits a few thousand years ago, not millions of years ago. The animals that could adapt lived; those that could not, died. Thus, survival, not evolution, explains the remaining animal life on Earth today.

When the world's sin problem is finally dealt with at the Second Coming of Jesus Christ, the curse on creation because of sin will be removed. Then there will not only be peace on earth and good will among men, but there will be tranquility within the animal kingdom as well (Rom. 8; Isa. 11). "And God said, Let us make man in our image, after our likeness. . . . So God created man in his own image, in the image of God created he him; male and female created he them" (Gen. 1:26–27).

As God is a trinity, man is a tri-part being—body, soul, and spirit. God commanded the first man and woman to multiply. From Adam and Eve, men and women have received forty-six chromosomes in each cell with some three million genes; over one hundred thousand have been catalogued. Genetically, Adam and Eve are represented in everyone's genes today, regardless of race (Acts 17:26). Our chromosomes predetermine our sex, physique, and to some extent, personality features. Even the number of hairs on our head is determined at conception (Ps. 139:13–17; Luke 12:7).

God ordained that all living things are created to reproduce their own kind, but He gave commandments only to man. He gave animals and insects the intelligence or instincts to survive in their own environment. Even squirrels and ants know to lay up food for the long winter months, which is more than some people do. Eagles have been observed dropping terrapins from several hundred feet on rocks to burst the shells, and even a fierce alligator will guard her eggs and protect her young. When men refuse to heed the commandments of God and depart from His will and purpose for their lives, then their knowledge and intelligence lead to their own destruction (Rom. 1).

Man was created on the sixth day, and six is the number of man (Rev. 13:18). According to biblical chronology, man was created six thousand years ago. The present human population of earth is six billion. Psalm 90 and Second Peter 3 relate that one day with God is as a thousand years, and many who study eschatology believe that man's day is up. God rested on the seventh day, so it may be that the Lord's Day is at hand.

The psalmist asked God to answer a question: "What

is man, that thou art mindful of him?" (Ps. 8:4).

The question is answered in the following psalm: To praise the Creator, to love his God, to keep the Lord's commandments. We come again to the ultimate answer to the creation of Adam and Eve in the Garden of Eden. God will have his own from among the millions of men and women who lived and died since the sixth creation day who will honor Him, praise Him, and serve Him for all eternity, not because they had to, but because they chose to in spite of all trials, temptations, and wiles of the Devil. This is the only honor and glory that man can bring to his Creator.

Man has built roads, cities, towers, ships, automobiles, and even walked on the moon. But God did not create man to build roads, cities, towers, ships, automobiles, or walk on the moon. These things by which man has sought to erect his own kingdom on earth will be destroyed (2 Pet. 3:10). God has an eternal kingdom, which is far greater than China, the United States, Russia, or Japan awaiting for those who have been saved according to His purpose (John 3:16; Dan 2:44; Eph. 3:9–10; Rev. 22).

A few of the examples of man and the number six biblical associations are as follows:

1. MAN was created on the SIXTH day (Gen. 1:27,31).
2. Revelation 13:18 says that 666 is "the number of a man."
3. The Bible has 66 books: it was written for MAN.

4. Genesis 6 has the word MAN mentioned SIX times.

5. Galatians 6 has the word MAN mentioned SIX times.

6. Second Chronicles 6 has the word MAN mentioned SIX times.

7. The following are interesting facts about the book of Joshua:

   a. It is the SIXTH book.

   b. It is the first book named after a MAN.

   c. Joshua has SIX letters.

   d. It has twenty-four chapters (4 x 6).

   e. "Men" is found SIX times in chapter SIX.

   f. Israel marched around Jericho for SIX days in chapter SIX.

   g. MAN is found SIX times in chapter SIX; thirty times in the whole book (5 x 6).

8. The following are interesting facts about Romans:

   a. It is the SIXTH book in the New Testament.

   b. The name of the book has SIX letters.

   c. The name has "MAN" in it; "Romans" means "an emphasis on MAN."

   d. MAN is the SIXTH word in Romans 6:6.

   e. SIX different times, MAN is the SIXTH word in a verse; the SIXTH time is in Romans 6:6 (also Romans 2:1, 3, 6; 3:28; 5:7; 6:6).

9. MAN is found two thousand six hundred and four times in the King James, exactly 434 x 6!

10. "Son of Man," with reference to Christ, is found eighty-four times, 14 x 6. FOURTEEN is the number of DELIVERANCE.

11. Man is born with a mortal body, and "mortal" is mentioned six times in the Bible (Job 4:17; Rom. 6:12; 8:11; 1 Cor. 15:53–54; 2 Cor. 4:11).

12. Fire and brimstone of Hell is reserved for men who die in their sins. Fire and brimstone is mentioned six times in the Bible.

13. The replica that Nebuchadnezzar made of his dream image, which represented the king's plan for man's empires, was six cubits wide and sixty cubits high (Dan. 3).

14. Goliath's height was six cubits and a span, and his spearhead weighed six hundred shekels of iron.

15. David and his men killed six giants, and one giant had six fingers on his hands and six toes on his feet.

16. The six manifestations of Jesus Christ as the Son of Man are:
    a. God was manifest in the flesh.
    b. Justified in the Spirit.
    c. Seen of angels.
    d. Preached unto the Gentiles.
    e. Believed on in the world.
    f. Received up into glory (1 Tim. 3:16).

17. Jesus Christ as the Son of Man will reign on earth for one thousand years. The thousand-year reign is mentioned six times in Revelation 20.

18. The walls on the New Jerusalem will be according to the "measure of a man," one hundred forty-four cubits high, or 24 x 6. There will be twelve gates to the city, 2 x 6.

Man was created by God on the sixth day; he was to work six days without rest; he reaches maturity at thirty years, or 5 x 6; he is appointed to die at the end of six decades, and after that, the judgment.

However, men and women who have received pardon from sin through faith in the blood of Jesus Christ Who died for sin, will not come into judgment, but receive the gift of eternal life (Eph. 2:1–10).

TGIS—
Thank God It's Saturday

We are informed at the beginning of the Bible that God rested on the seventh day. The seventh was sanctified as the Sabbath. In remembrance of God's miraculous works of creation, under the law, Israel was to likewise do no work on the Sabbath. The Gentile Saturday, or Saturn Day, was to honor the Roman god of agriculture. Inasmuch as we Gentiles use the Roman calendar, we also name the days of our week as the Romans did, to honor the pantheon gods lest they get angry and the oregano bushes produce no oregano.

The Jews demand a sign (1 Cor. 1:22), and the Sabbath was given to the Jews for a sign. A sign of what? As we read in Hebrews, the Sabbath was a sign to Israel that God would fulfill His promise in the Kingdom age, Millennium, a thousand-year era (one day is as a thousand years, Ps. 90) in which all the covenants with the nation would be fulfilled. I have been to Israel over forty times. On the Sabbath it is somewhat frustrating to eat cold, boiled eggs and bread, and then get in a Sabbath elevator that will stop at every floor before I arrive at the fortieth floor where my room is located.

The Gentile world had a Saturday, but not the Sabbath, and in no church conference mentioned in Acts, or the letters to the churches, is there any reference to Gentile Christians keeping the Sabbath. The Sabbath represented a promise of God to Israel. There are some Christians (mainly Seventh-Day Adventists) and messianic Jews who try to keep Saturday in some manner as the Jews did in Bible times. It has always been my contention that keeping Saturday or Sunday as a day of rest, or the Lord's Day, is not as important as how the Christian lives the other six days. If some Christians would want to keep February 29 as the Lord's Day, a day of gathering, fellowship and worship, that would be fine with me as long as they presented a commendable testimony the one thousand four hundred sixty days between February 29 and the next February 29.

But the patterns of sevens woven through Scripture was established in Genesis 2:2 when God rested on the seventh day. On the seventh day when God rested, He saw that everything He had created was good; therefore, seven is the perfect number. There are thousands of patterns of sevens in the sixty-six books of the Bible. I do not have the time to trace all these patterns, and the reader would not have time to read nor assimilate the information even if I did have the time. Some have tried, but the bits and pieces of information are so incomplete that we only get a glimpse of the miraculous mind of the Holy Spirit in directing the men who wrote the Scriptures. Therefore, I will trace the patterns and designs of numerical construction of sevens in the first book of the Bible, Genesis, the Gospels, and then the last book of the Bible, Revelation:

1. God rested on the seventh day of creation (Gen. 2:2).
2. God asked Adam a question in seven words, "Who told thee that thou wast naked?" (Gen. 3:11).
3. God asked Eve a question in seven words, "What is this that thou hast done?" (Gen. 3:13).
4. God's sentence upon the serpent was in sixty-three words, 9 x 7 (Gen. 3:14–15).
5. God protected Cain's life with a sevenfold judgment (Gen. 4:24).
6. Seven of each of the clean beasts was taken into the ark of Noah (Gen. 7:2).
7. God delayed the flood for seven days to give men a last opportunity to be saved (Gen. 7:4).
8. The Ark landed on the seventh month (Gen. 8:4).
9. Noah waited seven days before sending a dove to find land (Gen. 8:10).
10. Noah waited another seven days before sending another dove (Gen. 8:12).
11. Japheth had seven sons (Gen. 10:2).
12. Abraham bound his covenant with Abimelech with seven lambs (Gen. 21:28).

13. Jacob worked seven years for Rachel (Gen. 29:20).

14. Jacob worked another seven years for Rachel (Gen. 29:30).

15. Laban pursued Jacob for seven days (Gen. 31:23).

16. Jacob bowed to Esau seven times (Gen. 33:3).

17. In the dream of Pharaoh interpreted by Joseph there were:

    a. Seven fat cattle.

    b. Seven lean cattle.

    c. The seven lean cattle ate the seven fat cattle.

    d. Seven ears of corn on one stalk.

    e. Seven thin ears of corn.

    f. The seven thin ears ate the full ears.

    g. Seven years of plenty.

    h. Seven years of famine.

18. Bilhah, Rachel's maid, had seven sons from Jacob (Gen. 46:25).

19. Joseph mourned for his father, Jacob, seven days (Gen. 50:10).

As we proceed in the Old Testament the patterns of seven continue regardless of the subject or human recorder. In the Tabernacle, and later in the Temple, the measurements, sacrifices, and items of furniture that are numbered with sevens are amazing. But let us skip over to the Gospels and see if the seven designs at the first advent of Jesus Christ continued. If so, then this would be added evidence that He was and is the Messiah, the very Son of God:

1. From Abraham to David was fourteen generations, 2 x 7 (Matt. 1:17).
2. From David to the Babylonian captivity was fourteen generations, 2 x 7 (Matt. 1:17).
3. From the Babylonian captivity until Jesus Christ was fourteen generations, 2 x 7 (Matt. 1:17).
4. Jesus told the parable of the seven unclean spirits (Matt. 12:45).
5. Jesus fed above four thousand with seven loaves of bread (Matt. 15:34).
6. There were seven baskets of food left over (Matt. 15:37).
7. Jesus said we were to forgive a brother seventy times seven (Matt. 18:22).
8. The Sadducees tested Jesus with the wife who had seven husbands (Matt. 22:26).
9. Jesus cast seven devils out of Mary Magdalene (Mark 16:9).
10. Anna, a prophetess, lived with her husband seven years (Luke 2:36).
11. The nobleman's son was healed by Jesus at the seventh hour (John 4:52).
12. Jesus sent seventy disciples (10 x 7) to spread the gospel of the kingdom (Luke 10:1).

There are many other patterns of sevens in the Gospels as noted by E. W. Bullinger in his book on biblical numerics, but the preceding illustrations should be sufficient to prove that the numerical design in Scripture was carried over and continued from the Old Testament into the New Testament. This in itself is sufficient proof that the New Testament is also divinely inspired of God.

Next, let us consider the numerical patterns of sevens in the Book of Revelation:

1. There are seven churches of Asia (Rev. 1:4).
2. There are seven spirits of God before His throne (Rev. 1:4).
3. John saw seven golden candlesticks (Rev. 1:12).
4. John saw seven stars in the Lord's right hand (Rev. 1:16).
5. John saw seven angels of the seven churches (Rev. 1:20).
6. John saw seven lamps of fire (Rev. 4:5).
7. John saw a book sealed with seven seals (Rev. 5:1).
8. John saw a lamb with seven horns and seven eyes (Rev. 5:6).
9. John saw seven angels with seven trumpets (Rev. 8:2).
10. John heard seven thunders (Rev. 10:3).
11. An earthquake kills seven thousand men (Rev. 11:13).
12. John saw a red dragon with seven crowns on seven heads (Rev. 12:3).
13. John saw a beast rise out of the sea with seven heads (Rev. 13:1).
14. John saw seven angels with the seven last plagues (Rev. 15:1).

15. To the seven angels were given seven vials of the wrath of God (Rev. 15:6).
16. John saw a scarlet woman sitting on seven mountains (Rev. 17:9).
17. There were seven kings over world empires (Rev. 17:10).

Again, I present the evident fact that some forty writers of the Bible, living over a time span of some sixteen centuries, could not have continued an intricate and complicated mathematical design unless they had been guided by a Master Mathematician from Genesis to Revelation.

The message of Revelation is: "Behold, he cometh with clouds; and every eye shall see him, and they also which pierced him: and all kindreds of the earth shall wail because of him. Even so, Amen" (Rev. 1:7).

Jesus Christ is coming back, not to destroy the earth, but to destroy them which would destroy the earth (Rev. 11:18).

The invitation to the world extended by Jesus in the last chapter of Revelation is: "And, behold, I come quickly; and my reward is with me, to give every man according as his work shall be" (Rev. 22:12).

The last words of Jesus Christ recorded in the Bible are: "SURELY I COME QUICKLY" (Rev. 22:20).

Eight—
It Ain't Over 'Til It's Over

Seven is the perfect number, or the number of completion; therefore, if another number follows seven, then it must be the number of beginning again. Mathematics would be rather dull and limited if there were only seven numbers, and wouldn't life be rather limited and fearful if there were no second chance or new beginning.

Yogi Berra, the colorful catcher of the New York Yankees for several years, said of his team's chances in a world series, "It ain't over 'til it's over." Another expression is, "It isn't over until the fat lady sings." But even the fat lady has to start over when she sings: Do, Re, Mi, Fa, So, La, Ti, Do. After the seventh note, Ti, there is nowhere to go except back to Do, the eighth note. So even in music, eight is the number of a new beginning.

1. Eight persons were saved from the Flood to begin a new human order on earth.

2. Noah's name is found fifty-six times in the Bible, or 7 x 8.

3. Beginning with Abraham, Hebrew babies have been circumcised on the eighth day to signify they are heirs of God's covenants with Abraham, Isaac, and Jacob.

4. The word "alive" is found eighty-eight times in the Bible, 11 x 8.

5. The word "liveth" is found ninety-six times in the Bible, 8 x 12.

6. Reconciliation is found eight times in the Bible.

7. Redeem is found fifty-six times in the Bible, 8 x 7.

8. Revive is found eight times in the Bible.

9. Jesus is the "first fruits" of the first resurrection, and "first fruits" is found thirty-two times in the Bible, 4 x 8.

10. The word "salvation" is found one hundred four times in the Bible, 13 x 8.

11. Jesus was raised on the eighth day, which also is the first day of the week.

12. The disciples met on the eighth day, or the first day of the week.

13. The number eight is found eighty times in the Bible, 10 x 8.

14. Newborn animals given for sacrificial redemption from sin were to be given to God on the eighth day (Exod. 22:30).

According to E. W. Bullinger in *Numbers in Scripture* (pg. 201), the number of Jesus' Name in Greek is 888:

$$
\begin{aligned}
\text{I} &= 10 \\
\text{H} &= 8 \\
\Sigma &= 200 \\
\text{O} &= 70 \\
\Psi &= 400 \\
\Sigma &= \underline{200} \\
&\ 888
\end{aligned}
$$

Eight is identified many other times in Scripture as the number of a new beginning, being born again by faith in Jesus Christ. Jesus said, "I give unto them eternal life, and they shall never perish."

Those who have been born again ain't never going to hear the fat lady sing. The life we have in Jesus Christ is eternal; it will continue forever and ever when in the eighth dispensation we reign with our Lord in the New Heavens and the New Earth.

Nine Apples and Oranges

One of the cardinal rules of subject presentation is not to mix apples and oranges, which means: stick with the subject. However, the number nine in scripture not only has a reference to mixing fruit, but also to judgments, testings, and discipleship.

Nevertheless, the number nine's initial association is with fruit bearing, and not only to fruit or grain, but babies as well. In Genesis 1:28, God commanded the first man and the first woman, "Be fruitful and multiply." Christians are encouraged to "bear fruit" nine times in the Bible. Abraham was ninety-nine years old when he fathered a son by Sarah. On the Day of Pentecost today, members of the kibbutz in Israel bring the first fruits of the grain crops, the first fruits of the fruit trees, and the babies that have been born the previous year.

Jesus Christ died at the ninth hour, but He arose to become the first fruits of the first resurrection. In Galatians 5:22–23, the nine fruits of the Holy Spirit are given as: love, joy, peace, longsuffering, gentleness, goodness, faith, meekness, and temperance.

The total of 1611, the publishing date of the King

James Version, is $1+6+1+1=9$; there are nine letters in King James; and nine in Galatians, $5+2+2=9$.

Nine is also the number of judgments God brings for sinful rebellion. Judgment falls on: the land; the mountains; the corn; new wine; the oil; grass; men; cattle; and anything produced by man's labor (Hag. 1:11).

Because of sinful disobedience, the first Temple was destroyed on the ninth day of Av, 586 B.C.; because of rejecting their Messiah, Israel's second Temple was destroyed on the ninth day of Av, A.D. 70. The ninth of Av is observed as a day of mourning in Israel.

There are nine beatitudes in Jesus' Sermon on the Mount, and seven men are named who lived over nine hundred years. There are many events in Scriptures, both good and bad, blessings and curses, which are associated with the number nine. As indicated at the beginning, the number nine can be considered a mixed bag. But what an Omnipotent, Almighty Creator He must be to have created millions of interdependent life forms and have them to conform to the singleness of His purpose.

Ten—Enough Is Enough

The number ten in Scripture signifies the completion of God's Divine Order, or the finishing of His ordained will and purpose. Just a few of the hundreds of biblical examples where the number ten is used to illustrate the conclusion of the Divine cycle are as follows:

1. The tenth generation of Noah completed the Antediluvian age.
2. There were ten plagues on Egypt.
3. Under the Law a tithe (tenth) of one's increase was given to the Lord.
4. In the Tribulation the Antichrist will get his power from a ten-nation alliance.
5. Ten virgins were waiting for the bridegroom.
6. Ten things that cannot separate the Christian from salvation in Jesus Christ (Rom. 8:38–39): death, life, angels, principalities, powers, things present, things to come, heights, depth, nor any other creature.
7. The ten "I am's" of Jesus:
   a. I am the bread of life (John 6:35).
   b. I am the bread which came down from heaven

(John 6:41).

c. I am the living bread (John 6:51).

d. I am the light of the world (John 8:12).

e. I am one that bear witness of myself (John 8:18).

f. I am the door of the sheep (John 10:7).

g. I am the good shepherd (John 10:14).

h. I am the resurrection, and the life (John 11:25).

i. I am the way, the truth, and the life (John 14:6).

j. I am the true vine (John 15:1,5).

8. Ten categories of sinners who will be excluded from the Kingdom of God (1 Cor. 6:9–10): fornicators, idolaters, adulterers, effeminate, abusers of themselves, thieves, the covetous, drunkards, revilers, and extortioners.

9. Ten psalms that begin with "praise ye the Lord": Psalms 106, 111, 112, 113, 135, 146, 147, 148, 149, and 150.

10. According to Jewish records, nine red heifers have been sacrificed. When the tenth red heifer is sacrificed, the Messiah will come.

If ten plagues were not enough to deliver Israel, then God would have destroyed the nation of Egypt. If Ten Commandments are not enough to expose the sinfulness of sin, then a thousand wouldn't. In revealing His will and purpose to man, God has said that ten times over is enough—man is left without excuse (Rom. 1:20).

Eleven—
Here Comes the Judge

The biblical, numerical pattern of the number eleven in Scripture shows that it is the number of judgment. In Genesis 11, we find the judgment of Babel. In reference to Hell or judgment, "fire and brimstone" are connected in eleven different scriptures.

There were ten plagues upon Egypt, but the eleventh plague was outside of Egypt when Pharaoh's army was drowned in the Red Sea. At the Great White Throne Judgment, John saw eleven things happening:

1. He saw a great white throne.
2. He saw Him that sat on the throne.
3. He saw the dead, small and great, stand before God.
4. The books were opened.
5. Another book, the Book of Life, was opened.
6. The dead were judged out of things written in the books.
7. The sea gave up its dead.
8. Death and Hell delivered up their dead.

9. Every man was judged according to their works.
10. He saw Death and Hell cast into the lake of fire.
11. Those not written in the Book of Life were cast into the lake of fire.

There were eleven dukes of Edom, descendants of Esau, father of the Edomites. God pronounced everlasting judgment upon the Edomites (Exod. 17:16; Jer. 49:7; Ezek. 25:14; Joel 3:19).

Jehoiakim reigned for eleven years over Judah. He was killed for failing to obey Nebuchadnezzar of Babylon. Jehoiakim took a knife and deleted from a scroll the Words of God that he didn't like. He suffered a terrible death. The destruction of Jerusalem began at the end of his reign.

Zedekiah was the last king of Judah before Jerusalem and the Temple were destroyed. His sons were killed before him, and then he was blinded so that he would remember the last terrible scene he saw. Zedekiah reigned for eleven years.

Delilah betrayed Samson to the Philistines for eleven hundred pieces of silver (Judges 16:5).

An idol made of eleven hundred shekels of silver introduced idolatry to Israel in the time of the judges. Idol worship brought God's judgment upon the nation (Judges 17:1–6).

As previously noted, ten is God's number of completion and perfection of His ordained will. According to Revelation 22:18, if any person tries to add to what God has already ordained, commanded, written, or willed, God will judge that person. Eleven is one more than ten; thus, it is the number of judgment.

Eve tried to add to what God said. Her embellishment helped to bring sin on the entire human race. Let us beware of trying to either take from, or add to, God's Word. If we do, then we can be sure, as the comedian Flip Wilson used to say on his TV show that aired in the 1970s: "Here comes the Judge."

God Has No Baker's Dozen

When the wife shops she usually buys by the dozen: a dozen eggs, a dozen donuts, etc.

In the past generation it was common practice to put in an extra ear of corn or an extra donut. Giving an extra item was considered good PR. But when God says a dozen, He means twelve, not thirteen. God ordained government for a special reason: order, the punishment of criminals, the protection of the innocent, to protect the nation against foreign aggression (Gen. 9:1–7; Dan. 4:17; Rom. 13:1–7; 1 Tim. 2:1–7).

1. Ishmael would produce twelve nations (Gen. 17:20).
2. From Jacob would come twelve tribes of Israel (Gen. 49:28).
3. Twelve is a prominent number in the measurements and furnishings of both the Tabernacle and the Temple.
4. Jesus offered Israel the Kingdom of Heaven, and He chose twelve apostles to sit upon twelve thrones (Luke 22:30).

5. Israel rejected the kingdom offer, so God chose an apostle, Paul, to take the gospel to the Gentiles.
6. The twelve apostles will reign with Jesus Christ in the New Jerusalem where there are:
   a. Twelve gates.
   b. Twelve angels guarding the gates.
   c. Names of the twelve tribes of Israel on the twelve gates.
   d. Walls of the city have twelve foundations.
   e. The names of the twelve apostles will be on the twelve foundations.
   f. The New Jerusalem will be twelve thousand furlongs square.
   g. The twelve gates will be twelve pearls.
7. In the New Jerusalem there will be the Tree of Life bearing twelve different fruits for the twelve months of the year.
8. In The Tribulation period, twelve thousand from each of the twelve tribes of Israel will be sealed by God.
9. There are twelve constellations in the zodiac, signifying that God not only rules over men and nations, but He also rules over the heavens.
10. There are twelve months in the year, and the earth circles the sun every twelve months.
11. The Kingdom of God is a Divine government, and there are twenty-four members (2 x 12) in a heavenly senate (Rev. 4:4).
12. jesus went up to Jerusalem when He was twelve years old (Luke 2:42).

In the one hundred eighty-eight references to the number twelve in the Bible, twelve is associated with either temporal or heavenly government in the majority. For the forty or more writers living in different times over a span of sixteen hundred years, to have carried out this numerical design is just another example how they were directed by a Master Mathematician.

Going to
the Thirteenth Floor

In most hotels at home and abroad there are no thirteenth floors. Many people expect something bad has to happen on Friday the 13th. Possibly the reason is that in the Bible the number thirteen is given a rather bad rap. The first scripture where thirteen is referenced is Genesis 14:4 where the cities of the south rebelled against Chedorlaomer, king of Elam. From Genesis 14 to the Book of Revelation, thirteen is generally associated with sin and rebellion.

1. Genesis 13:13 says, "But the men of Sodom were wicked and sinners before the LORD exceedingly." THIRTEEN words!
2. In Genesis 13, Lot pitched his tent toward Sodom.
3. REBELLION is found in Genesis 13:13, First Samuel 13:13, Isaiah 13:13, Jeremiah 13:13, Deuteronomy 13:13, Mark 13:13, Ezekiel 13:13, and Revelation 13:13.
4. Deuteronomy 13 contains the rules for identifying a

false prophet whose miracles come to pass. In Revelation 13:13 the false prophet of the Tribulation period causes fire to come down out of Heaven in the sight of men.

5. Deuteronomy 13:13 contains the first reference to the "children of Belial."

6. First Kings 13 relates the story of a REBELLIOUS prophet. Verse 26 (2 x 13) gives the reason for his apostasy (REBELLION against the Word of the Lord).

7. Second Samuel 13 tells the story of Amnon, son of David, who raped his sister, Tamar. The chapter has thirty-nine verses (3 x 13).

8. "REBELLION" is the twenty-sixth word (2 x 13) in Ezra 4:19.

9. Revelation 17:5 has thirteen words in block capitals: MYSTERY, BABYLON THE GREAT, THE MOTHER OF HARLOTS AND ABOMINATIONS OF THE EARTH.

10. Mark 7:21–22 enumerates thirteen things which Jesus said proceeded from the depraved heart of man: evil thoughts, adulteries, fornications, murders, thefts, covetousness, wickedness, deceit, lasciviousness, an evil eye, blasphemy, pride, and foolishness.

11. John 13:26 (13:2 x 13) says, "Jesus answered, He it is, to whom I shall give a sop, when I have dipped it. And when he had dipped the sop, he gave it to Judas Iscariot, the son of Simon." Judas Iscariot has thirteen letters!

12. Psalm 55:13 contains a prophecy about Judas: "But it was thou, a man mine equal, my guide, and mine acquaintance." This verse has thirteen words.
13. The language of Micah 7:5 is a similar reference to this one whom Jesus called "friend" (Matt. 26:50). "Friend" and "guide" are connected in the verse; "guide" is the thirteenth word; the verse has twenty-six words (2 x 13).
14. Job 26:13 (2 x13:13) says, "By his spirit he hath garnished the heavens; his hand hath formed the crooked serpent." See Genesis 3:1. There is a thirteen-star CROOKED SERPENT between the Big Dipper and Little Dipper.
15. 666 is associated with thirteen (2 Chron. 9:13; Ezra 2:13; Rev. 13:18).
16. Nimrod is the thirteenth from Adam (Gen. 10:6–8).
17. According to Ezekiel 4:4–5, the years of apostasy for Israel's ten northern tribes were three hundred ninety, 13 x 30! The chapter and verses added come to thirteen (4+4+5=13).
18. Galatians 3:13 says, "Christ hath redeemed us from the curse of the law, being made a curse for us: for it is written, Cursed is every one that hangeth on a tree." CURSE is the last word in the Old Testament which has thirty-nine books (3 x 13).
19. Thirteen and thirteenth are referenced twenty-six (2 x 13) times in the Bible.

Friday is the sixth day of the week, and six is the number of man. The number thirteen is identified with sin and rebellion, and by one man sin was passed to all men (Rom. 5:12–13). Even if the thirteenth floor is labeled as the fourteenth floor, it is still the thirteenth floor. Even though sin may be called an error, mistake, or an inappropriate event, it is still sin. But Jesus Christ can cleanse us from all sin (1 John 1:7). Let the number thirteen be a reminder to put your faith and trust in Jesus Christ.

Pick a Number

We again stress the fact that it would be difficult to find a book in the world that has more numbers in it than the Bible. These numbers alone would indicate that this is not a book of myths, traditions, or conspiracy, and was so defended by the Apostle in Second Peter 1:16–21. Numbers verify and document, and even more so when numerical designs and patterns are continued by forty men living in different times over sixteen hundred years. We also should remember that until the Septuagint (and many dispute that there ever was a Septuagint), the Old Testament books were individual books. Also, the books of the Bible as we have them in the Authorized Version were not bound in one volume until after A.D. 300.

In this book the first thirteen numbers have been presented in their biblical designs and meanings. We continue and study the meanings and patterns of just a few of the more significant numbers:

Fifteen

Fifteen is associated with deliverance from death or peril:

1. The Ark of Noah bore eight souls through the Flood as the waters rose fifteen cubits above the highest mountain.

2. The Jews were delivered from the sentence of death in Persia on the fifteenth day of the month (Esther 9:18,21).

3. Hezekiah was granted an additional fifteen years to live (2 Kings 20:6).

4. Jesus raised Lazarus from the dead in Bethany, fifteen furlongs from Jerusalem.

5. The ship bearing Paul anchored fifteen fathoms, and the crew and passengers survived the storm.

Twenty-two

Twenty-two is the number of revelation. The following words are found twenty-two times in the Bible:

Brightness
Discovered
Learned
Known
Mystery
Tribulation

Thirty

Thirty, thirtieth, and thirty-fold are referenced one hundred eighty-five times in the Bible. There are many different associations with the number thirty, but the overriding one seems to be giving something in return for forgiveness, redemption, or atonement.

Joseph was sold for twenty shekels of silver, but he was only a teenager. The going price for a slave was thirty shekels of silver. Jesus was betrayed to the high priest for thirty pieces of silver, the price of a slave (Zech. 11:12–13; Matt. 26:15).

If an animal injured a person, the owner was to pay to the injured party thirty pieces of silver to atone for the damage.

John the Baptist, who baptized for the remission of sin (not forgiveness), began his ministry to announce the coming of the Messiah when he was thirty years of age. No Jew could hold a political or religious office until they reached the age of thirty.

Jesus began His public ministry at the age of thirty to offer evidence of His Messiahship (Luke 3:23).

Joseph was thirty years of age when he was made a high official of Pharaoh (Gen. 41:46).

David was thirty years of age when he began to reign as King of Israel (2 Sam 5:4).

The thirty pieces of silver that Judas received for betraying Jesus was called "the price of blood" (Matt. 27:4,6). "In whom we have redemption through his blood, the forgiveness of sins, according to the riches of his grace" (Eph. 1:7).

In the numbers of the Bible, God reminds us of so many wonderful truths. The next time you date a letter or a check, remember it was this many days ago that God sent His only begotten Son into the world to die for your sins in your place. Especially remember when you write a date with the thirtieth of the month, that we have redemption through His blood. What a wonderful Master Mathematician.

Forty

Forty is one of the more definitive numbers in Scripture as far as meaning is concerned. Forty means testing, probation, or proving. One of the numeric books I used for research stated that forty was mentioned one hundred sixty times in the Bible, which would be 4 x 40. My 1952 Royal is limited for computer research, so I counted all the numbers of forty, fortieth, or forties, and could come up with only one hundred fifty-nine—one hundred fifty verses, and in nine verses forty is mentioned twice. Maybe my *Strong's Concordance* missed one verse.

Forty is mentioned first in the Bible with judgment: ". . . I will cause it to rain upon the earth forty days and forty nights . . ." (Gen. 7:4).

Moses was in Egypt forty years; in Midian forty years; in the wilderness forty years (Acts 7:23,30; Exod. 16:35).

Forty days Moses was on the Mount to receive the Law (Exod. 24:18).

Forty years Israel wandered in the wilderness (Exod. 16:35).

Moses died at one hundred twenty years (3 x 40).

Jonah's message to Nineveh was, "Yet forty days, and Nineveh shall be overthrown" (Jonah 3:4).

This was a conditional prophecy; Nineveh repented and God withdrew His judgment.

Israel was given forty days to spy out the land (Num. 14:34).

David was king over Israel forty years (2 Sam. 5:4).

Solomon was king over Israel forty years (1 Kings 11:42).

Jesus was tempted forty days and forty nights by Satan (Luke 4:1–2).

Israel was given forty years to repent and cry out to God to send Jesus back before Jerusalem and the Temple were destroyed (Matt. 23:38; Acts 3:19–20).

Paul received forty stripes (save one) five times (2 Cor. 11:24).

There are many other references to testing, judgment, or warning of judgment, in the number forty from Genesis to Revelation, but the reader should get the idea in just these examples. Forty is another number that is consistent in pattern and design that proves the One Who guided the pen of the human writers of the Scriptures was indeed a Master Mathematician.

Before advancing to the next number of primary importance, we must consider the number thirty-eight. In John 5:5 we find a lame man who had been so afflicted thirty-eight years, waiting at the pool of Bethesda for the water to move. As the account relates, the man thought that if he could get into the water while it was moving he would be healed. In going by this pool today it is easy to see the difficulty. The pool was more than one hundred feet below ground level and could be reached only by going down five sets of stairs.

Israel was two years on the way to the Promised Land. They wandered in the wilderness for thirty-eight years until that generation died—with the exception of two men. The lame man represented Israel who could only be healed of unbelief through faith in Jesus Christ as their Messiah.

Fifty

Fifty in the Bible is the number of jubilee, interpreted as a time of shouting accompanied with the blowing of a trumpet, or shofar. The reason for the shouting is that the year of jubilee (Lev. 25:11) was the year of redemption. Jubilee was every fiftieth year, or seven sabbatical years. Every seventh year the land was to lay idle, and on the year after seven sabbatical years (forty-nine years), the land was to lay idle an extra year. This was also the year that land was to be returned to the original owner even if he had no money to buy it back. However, this redemption did not cover a house or home in the city—only lands outside the cities. The year of jubile was also a time for those outside of Israel to return to their families in the land. "And ye shall hallow the fiftieth year, and proclaim liberty throughout all the land unto all the inhabitants thereof: it shall be a jubile unto you; and ye shall return every man unto his possession, and ye shall return every man unto his family" (Lev. 25:10).

The number fifty, therefore, also held a promise of Israel's return to the land with the coming of Messiah. Fifty is also the number of resurrection and eternal life.

Pentecost came in Israel fifty days after the Passover. It was during this time that fruits and grain matured and the first fruits of the harvest were to be brought to the Lord. Jesus instructed the disciples to wait in Jerusalem for fifty days until Pentecost when the Holy Spirit would come to indwell in them. Jesus had ascended to the Father forty days after His resurrection, but ten days before Pentecost.

At Pentecost, on the first day of the week (our Sunday, not Saturday), the priest was to wave a sheaf of the grain crop before the Lord as the offering of first fruits (Lev. 23:9–11). This offering symbolized the future resurrection of Jesus Christ, the first fruits of the first resurrection (1 Cor. 15:23), who was raised on the first day of the week. The coming of the Holy Spirit at Pentecost was evidence of the acceptance by the Father of the offering of Jesus Christ, His only begotten Son, for sin. Therefore, the Holy Spirit could dwell in those who are purged from sin as His temple (1 Cor. 3:16; 6:19).

Fifty was a prominent number in the construction and dimensions of the Tabernacle and the Temple. We encourage the reader to study carefully how the pattern and design of fifty throughout the Bible speaks of the redemption and resurrection we have through faith in Jesus Christ. Again, I must say it: What a marvelous Master Mathematician God is.

Seventy

Seven is the number of perfection and ten is the number of completion. Therefore, seventy (10 x 7) is the number of perfect completion. This does not mean that seventy always connects with something that is perfectly good; it could refer to something that is perfectly evil.

I was surprised that Bullinger passed over this number with only a few references and comments, and Hoggard ignored it completely. It could be that the publisher editing is responsible, as a three-hundred page, fifteen dollar book on numerics will sell better than a thousand-page, thirty-dollar book on numerics.

To illustrate the meaning of seventy, a few biblical examples are listed:

1. Noah had seventy grandsons from which was to come seventy nations (Gen. 10).
2. Israel's captivity in Babylon was seventy years (Jer. 25:11–12; Dan. 9:2).
3. God's promises to Israel will be fulfilled in seventy weeks of years (Dan. 9).
4. Moses selected seventy men to assist him (Num. 11:16).
5. Jesus sent seventy disciples to declare the gospel of the Kingdom (Luke 10).
6. Seventy years from the birth of Jesus Christ Israel ceased to be a nation.
7. The righteous can expect a life span of seventy years (Ps. 90:10).

Some interpret a generation to be forty years, as forty is the number of testing or proving. Others think that seventy years is a generation based on man's fullest expected life-span. In the Olivet Discourse, the last generation referenced by Jesus covered the return of Israel to His Second Coming. This being true, the last generation would be more than forty years. If for the sake of conjecture we agree that the last generation would be seventy years, and Israel's refounding as a nation in 1948 the starting time, then Jesus would come back in 2018 and the Rapture of the church would occur in 2011. Again, this is only conjecture, because I do not know that Jesus is coming back in 2018, and other than God, no one knows. We do know that Jesus said we could know that His coming was near, even at the door. Right now, I am listening for that knock on the door.

One Hundred Twenty

While this number is mentioned only a few times in Scripture, it is a most interesting one. In the few scriptures where we find this number, it appears to be a number indicating a Divine waiting period. God gave the generation of Noah's day one hundred twenty years to repent of the evil and violence that beset it.

1. Those Israelite men who came out of Egypt numbered six hundred thousand, 120 x 5000.
2. The number of Jews returning from Babylon was forty-two thousand three hundred sixty, 120 x 353.
3. During the Tribulation, one hundred forty-four thousand Israelites will be sealed, 120 x 1,200.

We notice also that the number of disciples who were to wait for the coming of the Holy Spirit in Acts 1:15 was ABOUT one hundred twenty. As noted previously, exact numbering is a Kingdom age entity and generally does not apply to the Church age. Although some of my ministry brethren will doubtless contradict me with much wailing and gnashing of teeth, what tentative numbering there is in Acts and the Epistles indicated that the kingdom offer of Peter and John in Acts 3:19 was left open until the Temple was destroyed in A.D. 70.

Other Numbers

There are many other numbers in the Scripture that further evidence that only our God, the Master Mathematician, could have written the Bible. For example, the number sixty-six is the number of worship—either man himself, an idol, or the true God. Our Bible has sixty-six books. It is the authoritative Word of God for mankind. We will also study many of these numbers missed in a future chapter in this book about numbers in prophecy.

For those who would like to study further about biblical numerics, I recommend: *Number In Scripture,* by the late E. W. Bullinger; *Biblical Mathematics,* by the late Ed Vallowe; and *By Divine Order,* by the very much alive Michael Hoggard.

New Math Isn't New

The mathematical structure of Genesis 1 in the Hebrew text has already been discussed at some length, along with the imprint of the Master Mathematician. But consider also that seven times God said that what He created was "good": verses 4, 10, 12, 18, 21, 25, and 31. The verb "made" is also found seven times in regards to God's specific creative acts: 1:7, 16, 25, 26, 31; 2:2, 3. In Genesis 1, heaven is mentioned seven times: verses 1, 8, 9, 14, 15, 17, and 20. God Himself as Creator is mentioned thirty-five times, 5 x 7, in the Creation account from Genesis 1:1 to Genesis 2:4.

We read of the first day of Creation in Genesis 1:3–5:

> And God said, Let there be light: and there was light. And God saw the light, that it was good: and God divided the light from the darkness. And God called the light Day, and the darkness he called Night. And the evening and the morning were the first day.

Even on the first day of Creation we witness the operation of mathematical laws which govern the universe, set in motion by the Master Mathematician. In the sphere of light there are exactly seven colors. They merge together to form light. One is the number of God, for there is One God; and we read in the Bible that God is light, and in Him is no darkness (1 John 1:5). On the first day, God divided the light from the darkness.

We read in Genesis 1:6–8 that on the second day of Creation, God made the firmament, or atmosphere. Atmosphere contains the necessary elements for life, and without it, there would be neither animals nor plants. It contains oxygen, necessary for animal life, and carbon dioxide, necessary for plant life. Two is the number of witness, and these two elements bear witness that God is the Author of all life on earth, whether animal or vegetable.

In other words, animals did not evolve from plants or vice-versa. Without atmosphere, there would be no sound. In music, there are exactly seven whole tones in a scale, while every eighth note begins a new octave and is a repetition of the first note.

Of the third day Genesis 1:9–10 says:

And God said, Let the waters under the heaven be gathered together unto one place, and let the dry land appear: and it was so. And God called the dry land Earth; and the gathering together of the waters called he Seas: and God saw that it was good.

Water at first covered the entire planet, but on the third

day God divided the waters and the land. We now have seven continents: Europe, Asia, Africa, North America, South America, Australia, and Antarctica. God also gathered the waters into seas; and again, according to maritime terminology from the *Encyclopaedia Britannica,* we have seven seas: North Pacific, South Pacific, North Atlantic, South Atlantic, Indian Ocean, Arctic Ocean, and Mediterranean Sea.

We read further concerning the third day of creation:

> And God said, Let the earth bring forth grass, the herb yielding seed, and the fruit tree yielding fruit after his kind, whose seed is in itself, upon the earth: and it was so. And the earth brought forth grass, and herb yielding seed after his kind, and the tree yielding fruit, whose seed was in itself, after his kind: and God saw that it was good. And the evening and the morning were the third day.
>
> —Genesis 1:11–13

Numerical patterns in the plant or vegetable kingdom are numerous, and impossible to discuss in any detail in this brief study. The grains in Indian corn are set in rows and always arranged in even, never odd, numbers. Leaves are arranged upon a stem in perfect order so that one is exactly parallel to the first leaf on the stem. On the apple tree it is the fifth leaf, on the oak the fourth, on the peach the sixth, etc. In endogens (house plants), three is the prevailing number, while in exogens (outside plants), five is the prevailing number. Every acorn, every fruit, every leaf, every blade of grass grows in an exact mathematical design.

Of the fourth day of creation, Genesis 1:14,16 says:

> And God said, Let there be lights in the firmament of the heaven to divide the day from the night; and let them be for signs, and for seasons, and for days, and years. . . . And God made two great lights; the greater light to rule the day, and the lesser light to rule the night: he made the stars also.

A lunar month, the time it takes for the moon to circle around the earth, is twenty-eight days, or 4 x 7; the distance the moon is from the earth is two hundred thirty-eight thousand miles, or 34,000 x 7. The diameter of the moon is twenty-one hundred miles, or 300 x 7.

The sun, which also appeared on the fourth day, does not follow the creative pattern of seven. It fits into the numerical pattern for the Godhead, the number three. Perhaps the reason for the sun's place in this particular mathematical design is that without God the Creator there would be no life. Without the sun, all life on earth would become extinct within a matter of hours. God is also light; He made the sun to rule the day. The distance of our sun from the earth is ninety-three million miles, or 31,000,000 x 3. The relation of Newton's law of gravity between the sun and the earth is 2 x 10 gms to the

33rd power (11 x 3), or 2 x 10 tons to the 27th power (9 times 3). The sun's mass is three hundred thirty-three thousand times that of earth, or 111,000 x 3. Earth is the third planet from the sun. It circles the sun at the speed of sixty-six thousand miles an hour, or 22,000 x 3; our solar system has nine planets that revolve around the sun (3 x 3). The sun crosses the vernal (spring) equinox in the third month (March), the twenty-first day (7 x 3) and the autumnal equinox in September, the ninth month (3 x 3) on the twenty-first day (7 x 3).

In our study on the connection between the days of Creation and what was created on specific days, as well as related mathematical construction between the days and the Creation, we should also note the dispensational typology.

The First Day. This day typifies the first dispensation, the dispensation of innocence. Adam and Eve were clothed with light, and they walked in the light of God without sin.

The Second Day. God divided the waters between the earth and atmosphere. This was the environment that existed during the dispensation of conscience. Although mankind was banned from the Garden of Eden because of sin, there was no government-instituted penalty for sin. Man was protected here on earth and also from the life-shortening cosmic rays of the sun. At the end of the dispensation of conscience, the water above the firmament came down, resulting in the flood.

The Third Day. Dry land appeared on earth, and

the appearance of land after the flood signaled the beginning of the third dispensation: human government. At its conclusion, all land mass was broken up and the human race scattered over the face of the Earth.

The Fourth Day. On the fourth day God made the sun, moon, and stars to appear. In the fourth dispensation, the dispensation of the Law, God called one nation and committed them to the stewardship of His Word through the prophets and His Law whereby Israel could be brought to the position to bring forth a Savior to the world and restore the kingdom from Heaven to a rebel planet. In Revelation 12:1 Israel is described as a woman clothed with the sun, the moon under her feet, and stars on her head. God also made the moon, sun, and stars for prophetic signs. The writers of all Bible prophecies were Israelites; in fact, all the human authors of the books of the Bible were Israelites, with the possible exception of Luke.

The Fifth Day. God made fish and fowl forms of life. Five is the number of grace, and the fifth day typifies the dispensation of grace. At the birth of Jesus, Who came to bring mankind the salvation of God by grace, the sun passed into the Pisces constellation, the sign of the fish. Early Christians used this sign for identification purposes; Jesus multiplied five loaves and two fish to feed five thousand (John 6). The creation of the fowls to fly in the midst of Heaven may represent the calling out of this world a people for Christ's name to inhabit heavenly places with Him. This calling out is to occur during the dispensation of grace. The sun is now passing out of the sign of Pisces, the fish, and going into the sign of Aquarius, another indication that the dispensation of grace is about to end and the return of Jesus Christ is near.

The Sixth Day. God's creation on the sixth day (Gen. 1:24–27) included all other creatures—wild and domesticated animals, insects, and all other life that falls outside the insect kingdom. Last of all, God made man. As we have stated, six is the number of man, so declared in Revelation 13:18. A mathematical pattern is found throughout the life forms God created on the sixth day. The pattern of three and six is found throughout insects. For example, let us consider the bee:

- The worker grub matures in twenty-one days (7 x 3).
- It is at work three days after leaving the cell.
- The drone matures in twenty-four days (8 x 3).
- The bee is composed of three sections, head and two stomachs.
- The two eyes are made of approximately three thousand small eyes (1,000 x 3), with each eye having six sides (2 x 3).
- There are six wax scales underneath the bee (2 x 3).
- Like all insects, the bee has six legs (2 x 3).
- The egg of the queen bee is hatched in three days.
- It is fed for nine days (3 x 3).
- It reaches maturity in fifteen days (5 x 3).

The animal kingdom reintroduces the number seven.

The gestation period of just a few animals are as follows:

- The mouse is twenty-one days (3 x 7).
- The rabbit and the rat are twenty-eight days (4 x 7).
- The cat is fifty-six days (8 x 7).
- The dog is sixty-three days (9 x 7).
- The lion is ninety-eight days (14 x 7).
- The sheep is one hundred forty-seven days (21 x 7).
- Hen eggs are hatched in twenty-one days (3 x 7).
- Duck eggs hatch in forty-two days (6 x 7).
- The human species gestation period is two hundred eighty days (40 x 7).

The sixth day of creation represents man's day; six is the number of man. Man's day will be a period of seven years in which the world will be commanded to worship a man of its own choosing, a man with the number of man—666. Afterward, the Lord's Day will come, represented by the seventh day—a day of rest from war, famine, crime, disease, and sorrow. Throughout the Bible, mankind is promised this dispensational day of rest. According to the book *Number In Scripture*, there is medical evidence that man's pulse beats slower on the seventh day than the previous six days. This is a sign from God that man is to take one day to remember his Creator, and then look forward to that heavenly day of rest for all who are in Jesus Christ.

Looking for Your Star

There are millions of stars in our own galaxy, the Milky Way. Some of these stars are hundreds or thousands times bigger than our own sun. Then, there are millions of galaxies strung in space over millions of light years. Abraham was looking at the stars and concluded that someone infinitely greater than he was must have created all this. Because of that grain of faith, God revealed Himself to Abraham. Today, the best the so-called smartest minds can come up with is the "Big Bang" idea: billions of years ago a piece of matter the size of a pea suddenly exploded, and voila!—the universe appeared and began to spread outward. I think Abram, even though he never attended a day at MIT, was right. "And God said, Let there be lights in the firmament of the heaven to divide the day from the night; and let them be for signs, and for seasons, and for days, and years" (Gen. 1:14).

Later in this chapter we may pursue the reason why God created so many stars, but we note for our immediate attention that God created them for "signs." The word sign, or *oth,* has a prophetic or futuristic meaning.

If driving down the highway you saw a McDonald's sign, you could park by that sign for a year and not even one Big Mac would appear. What you have to do after you see the sign is start looking for the real establishment.

Josephus, the governor of Galilee who started the Jewish rebellion against Rome in A.D. 66, was commissioned by Rome to write a history of the Jews. Josephus was given the scrolls taken from the Temple by the Romans. Had the works of Josephus not been saved by Rome, they doubtless would have been destroyed. In *Antiquities of the Jews*, book 1, chapter 2, Josephus commented on the descendants of Seth and their understanding of heavenly signs:

> Now this Seth, when he was brought up, and came to those years in which he could discern what was good, became a virtuous man; and as he was himself of an excellent character, so did he leave children behind him who imitated his virtues. All these proved to be of good dispositions. They also inhabited the same country without dissensions, and in a happy condition, without any misfortunes falling upon them till they died. They also were the inventors of that peculiar sort of wisdom, which is concerned with the heavenly bodies, and their order. And that their inventions might not be lost before they were sufficiently known, upon Adam's prediction that the world was to be destroyed at one time by the force of fire, and at another time by the violence and quantity of

water, they made two pillars; the one of brick, the other of stone: they inscribed their discoveries on them both, that in case the pillar or brick should be destroyed by the flood, the pillar of stone might remain, and exhibit those discoveries to mankind; and also inform them that there was another pillar of brick erected by them. Now this remains in the land of Siriad to this day.

The land of Siriad was the area of Egypt located where the city of Cairo is today. The pillar of stone would have to be the Great Pyramid, or the Sphinx about four hundred yards from the Great Pyramid, or both.

There have been many books written about the Great Pyramid, including mine, *The Great Pyramid—Prophecy In Stone*. In doing further research on this subject recently, I noted that most pyramidologists suggested that based on the measurement in pyramid inches of the ascending passageway in the Great Pyramid, that this age would come to a screeching halt somewhere about A.D. 2000. One even gave the date of September 17, 2001. While I do not personally set dates for the Tribulation, appearance of the Antichrist, or the Second Advent, in consideration of chapter eleven on, "Here Comes the Judge," the reader might find the following statistical information related to the September 11, 2001, Twin Trade Towers catastrophe interesting:

♦ The day of the attack: 11
♦ The date of the attack, September 11 or 9/11 =

$9+1+1=11$

- 911 is emergency number $= 9+1+1=11$
- September 11 is the two hundred fifty-fourth day of the year: $2+5+4=11$
- After September 11 we have **111** days remaining for the end of the year
- 119 is the area code for Iran and Iraq $1+1+9=11$
- The first plane to hit one of the buildings was Flight **11**
- The state of New York was the **11**th state to join the Union
- New York City $=$ **11** letters
- Afghanistan $=$ **11** letters
- The Pentagon $=$ **11** letters
- Flight 11 had ninety-two passengers, $9+2=11$
- Flight 77 had sixty-five passengers, $6+5=11$
- Twin Towers look like an **11**
- Twin Towers had **110** floors

The Number of the Stars

Moses was directed by God to declare in Genesis 1:14–19 that God created the sun, moon, and stars. The Creator made them not only for light and seasons; He also made them for signs to mankind. The apostle Paul included the witness of the Creator to mankind in the stars in Romans 1:18–19: "For the wrath of God is revealed from heaven against all ungodliness and unrighteousness of men, who hold the truth in unrighteousness; Because that which may be known of God is manifest in them;

for God hath shewed it unto them."

God's witness to man in the stars is also stated in Psalm 19:1,3: "The heavens declare the glory of God; and the firmament sheweth his handiwork. . . . There is no speech nor language, where their voice is not heard."

We read also in Psalm 147:4: "He telleth the number of the stars; he calleth them all by their names."

Of the heavens' witness to the generation living in the last days, Jesus said in Luke 21:25: "And there shall be signs in the sun, and in the moon, and in the stars. . . ."

From the scriptural record we know that God not only named the sun and the moon, He also gave the billions of stars names and numbered them. In Job 9:9 three constellations are identified: Arcturus, Orion, and Pleiades. In other scriptures constellations and signs of the zodiac are mentioned (Job 38:32; 2 Kings 23:5; Isa. 13:10; Amos 5:8). In Acts 28:11 the sign of Gemini, the twins, are referred to; their ancient names were Castor and Pollux.

Signs of the zodiac as bearing testimony to the Creator and His will in both Heaven and Earth are not condemned in the Bible; however, the prostitution of these signs by astrologers is condemned (Isa. 47:13–14). There are twelve signs in the zodiac; twelve is the biblical number of government. Three is the number of the Godhead, and four is the number of earth—3 x 4 = 12. Twelve signs in the zodiac speak of God's rule over the universe. The Kingdom of Heaven ruled by God is government, or it would not be called a Kingdom. There are twelve tribes of Israel; twelve apostles; the New Jerusalem, the center of God's government will have twelve foundations and twelve gates; it will be twelve thousand furlongs square; the walls will be one hundred forty-four cubits high (12 x 12); twelve thousand Israelites will be sealed by God from each of the twelve tribes of Israel during the Tribulation. Once more, God, the Master Mathematician, has proven that He also created the heavens through the numerical design of His Word.

Each sign in a constellation is composed of many stars. The three brightest stars serve as markers. The ancients connected the stars with visionary lines and, with added imagination or revelation, formed living creatures and objects which told a story. Corruption of these signs in the heavens probably occurred after the flood, resulting in the false science of astrology. It is almost certain that Paul was referring to the signs of the zodiac being worshiped by the ancients in Romans 1:22–25:

> Professing themselves to be wise, they became fools,
> And changed the glory of the uncorruptible God into
> an image made like to corruptible man, and to birds,
> and fourfooted beasts, and creeping things. Where-
> fore God also gave them up to uncleanness through
> the lusts of their own hearts, to dishonor their own
> bodies between themselves: Who changed the truth
> of God into a lie, and worshipped and served the crea-
> ture more than the Creator, who is blessed for ever.
> Amen.

Signs of the zodiac are arranged in a circle. By looking at the face of a clock it is possible to visualize each of the twelve numbers standing for a different constellation. Earth would be at the extremity of the hour hand, which revolves around the center, the sun, every three hundred sixty-five and one-quarter days. The sun appears to travel through the signs, changing from one to another with each passing month.

Stars in our galaxy, the Milky Way, also revolve around a common center. If stars moved around the center like rigid spokes in a wheel, the earth would end up, in relation to the zodiac, at exactly the same spot every three hundred sixty-five and one-quarter days. Instead, stars move in a celestial circle, more like objects in a whirlpool, causing the sun to change one degree every seventy-one years. This is comparable to a clock losing about forty seconds a year. The effect is that the sun passes from one sign to another approximately every two thousand years, making the complete circle in twenty-five thousand five hundred seventy-nine years. This complete circuit is called the "Precession of the Equinoxes."

The ancients placed the starting point on the celestial clock at Virgo and the end at Leo. This order is seen in monuments of antiquity, like the Sphinx near the Great Pyramid of Giza: Virgo, the head of a maiden, and Leo, the lion, at the rear, signifying the beginning and the end. This is the riddle of the Sphinx.

It is impossible in this brief study of constellations

to discuss at any length the numerical composition arranged by the Creator, but briefly the biblical truth they represent is as follows:

1. **VIRGO, the Virgin.** The seed of woman to bring forth the Savior (Gen. 3:15): "Behold, a virgin shall conceive, and bear a son, and shall call his name Immanuel" (Isa. 7:14). Virgo contains one hundred ten stars—11 x 10. Ten is the number of perfect completion. In this constellation there is one star of the first magnitude, six of the third, and ten of the fourth. One is the number of God; six is the number of man; three is the number of the triune God—Father, Son, and Holy Spirit; four is the number of the world; and ten is the number of perfect completion. Herein lies the story of John 3:16, "For God so loved the world, that he gave his only begotten Son, that whosoever believeth in him should not perish, but have everlasting life."

2. **LIBRA, the Unbalanced Scales:** This constellation signifies the story of man's unsuccessful attempt to buy, or work for, his own salvation. "Thou art weighed in the balances, and art found wanting" (Dan. 5:27). At the Great White Throne Judgment, every man or woman who has not received the virgin-born Son of God as Savior will be judged, or weighed, according to their works, and all will be cast into the lake of fire (Rev. 20:11–15). This constellation has fifty-one stars. According to *Number In*

Scripture by E. W. Bullinger, fifty is the number of deliverance or jubilee; one is the number of God, making fifty-one the number of Divine revelation or deliverance. Of the fifty-one stars, two are of the second magnitude, one of the third, and eight of the fourth. Besides the numerical typology already given, two is the number of witness, and eight is the number of Jesus Christ. "For by grace are ye saved through faith; and that not of yourselves: it is the gift of God: Not of works, lest any man should boast. For we are his workmanship, created in Christ Jesus unto good works . . ." (Eph. 2:8–10).

3. **SCORPIO, the Scorpion:** The sting of sin to death that infects every man. There are forty-four stars in this constellation—included are one of the first magnitude, one of the second, eleven of the third, and eight of the fourth. Forty-four is 11 x 4, representing man's best effort. Concerning the meaning of eleven, we quote from *Number In Scripture:* "If ten is the number which marks the perfection of Divine order, then eleven is an addition to it, subversive of and undoing that order." We read in First Corinthians 15:56, "The sting of death is sin. . . ." ". . . For there is none other name under heaven given among men, whereby we must be saved" (Acts 4:12) and Revelation 22:18–19 states that if anyone attempts to add to or take from the words of God recorded in the Bible, and this certainly includes the way of salvation, his name will be taken out of the book of life.

4. **SAGITTARIUS, the Warrior:** The One who came to defeat the old serpent, the Devil, and who will come again to save the world from the Devil's anointed ruler, the Antichrist. There are sixty-nine stars in this sign and includes five of the third magnitude and nine of the fourth. Sixty-nine is a combining number, 10 x 6 + 9. Five is the number of grace, and nine is the number of rebellion. When Jesus Christ returns, the world will be in rebellion against God and His anointed; He will return as King of kings, and Lord of lords, leading the armies of Heaven to destroy those of Antichrist. As told in Zechariah 12:10, He will pour out the spirit of grace upon the house of David and Jerusalem.

5. **CAPRICORN, the Goat:** The goat was the atonement animal that pointed forward to the ultimate sacrifice that God would prepare. Hebrews 9:28; 10:4–5, says: "So Christ was once offered to bear the sins of many; and unto them that look for him shall he appear the second time without sin unto salvation. . . . For it is not possible that the blood of bulls and of goats should take away sins. Wherefore when he cometh into the world, he saith, Sacrifice and offering thou wouldest not, but a body hast thou prepared [for] me." Fifty-one stars are in this constellation, which includes three of the third magnitude and three of the fourth. As we have already presented, fifty-one is the number of Divine revelation. The three stars of the third magnitude and the three

of the fourth magnitude signify that Jesus Christ, who was sacrificed for us, was both perfect God, revealed in three persons, and perfect man, whom God sent into the world to save the world from the penalty of sin.

6. **AQUARIUS, the Water-Bearer:** The Sent One who would pour out waters of blessings on the Earth in the former and latter rain. Numbers 24:7, Isaiah 32:1–2, and many more scriptures prophesy that the Messiah would come to pour out upon the earth abundant waters of blessings upon the world and mankind. Joel prophesies that when He returns He will come as the latter rain to bring life to a dying earth (Joel 2:23). There are one hundred eight stars in this sign, which includes four of the third magnitude. One hundred eight is a combining number, 10 x 10 signifying ultimate perfection, the Blessed Hope of the world. Eight is the number of Jesus Christ.

7. **PISCES, the Two Fish:** The two fish that would be multiplied as a symbol of God's grace offered to the world. John 6 records that Jesus took two fish and fed five thousand people. Five is the number of grace. When Jesus Christ was born, the sun entered the sign of Pisces and is now passing into the sign of Aquarius. One of the fish in the sign is parallel to earth while the other points upward toward Heaven. We believe this signifies that God is calling out of this world a people for His name during this dispensation of grace to inherit heavenly places. Included

in this constellation are three other signs: the band binding the fish together; Cepheus, the king and redeemer coming to rule; and Andromeda, the chained woman, signifying Israel in bondage and affliction. There are one hundred fifty-three stars in all facets of this constellation, as far as we could determine, which we associate with the one hundred fifty-three fish the disciples caught when Jesus instructed them to cast their net on the right side of their ship. As brought out in our book *Apocalyptic Signs in the Heavens,* these represent one hundred fifty-three nations that Jesus Christ will catch up into His Kingdom when He returns. There are at least fourteen references in the Bible comparing this event to a fisherman catching fish in a net.

8. **ARIES, the Lamb:** The Lamb of God Who would take away the sins of the world. Isaiah prophesied that the Messiah would come as a lamb being led to the slaughter. John 1:29 says: "Behold the Lamb of God, which taketh away the sin of the world." There are sixty-six stars in this sign, one for each book in the Bible. The story of the Savior coming as the Lamb of God to shed His blood for the sins of the world binds all sixty-six books of the Bible together, from Genesis to Revelation.

9. **TAURUS, the Bull:** The Messiah coming to tread underfoot all who obey not the gospel. The bull in this sign is not as one being led to the sacrificial altar, but is a raging bull on the attack. There are

one hundred forty-one stars in this sign. This is a combining number, 10x10+40+1. One is the number of God and forty the number of testing or probation. When Jesus Christ comes again, man will have been given his last opportunity to set his own house in order.

10. **GEMINI, the Twins:** The twofold nature of the Messiah: Son of Man and Son of God. There are eighty-five stars in this sign, a combining number: 10 x 8 + 5. Ten is the number of completion and perfection: eight is the number of Jesus Christ; five is the number of grace. Perfect grace and truth came in the person of Jesus Christ.

11. **CANCER, the Crab:** Possessions held fast, the security of the children of God. Jesus said: "And I give unto them eternal life; and they shall never perish, neither shall any man pluck them out of my hand" (John 10:28). There are eighty-three stars in this sign, a combining number of 10 x 8 + 3. This number signifies the perfect Savior who brought perfect, not conditional, salvation.

12. **LEO; the Lion:** The Lion of the Tribe of Judah coming to reign forever. Luke 1:32–33 says: "He shall be great, and shall be called the Son of the Highest: and the Lord God shall give unto him the throne of his father David: And he shall reign over the house of Jacob for ever; and of his kingdom there shall be no end." In Revelation 5:5, Jesus as King of kings is identified as, ". . . the Lion of the tribe of Juda, the Root

of David." There are ninety-five stars in this sign, 9 x 10 + 5. While He will come to end all rebellion on earth and restore the kingdom from Heaven, He will reign in grace and mercy. As the Word of God declares, the Master Mathematician numbered the stars; He called them all by name so that the Bible in the heavens shows forth His glory in order that all are without excuse to come to the knowledge of the truth and be saved.

Dr. J. A. Seiss, noted theologian of the past century, stated in the first chapter of his extensive book, *The Gospel in the Stars:*

There can therefore be no full and right declaring of "the glory of God" which does not reach and embrace Christ, and the story of redemption through Him, but the starry worlds, simply as such, do not and cannot declare or show forth Christ as the Redeemer, or the glory of God in Him. If they do it at all, they must do it as "signs," arbitrarily used for that purpose. Yet the Psalmist affirms that these heavens do "declare the glory of God." Are we not therefore to infer that the story of Christ and redemption is somehow expressed by the stars? David may or may not have so understood it, but the Holy Ghost, speaking through him, knew the implication of the words, which, in such a case, must not be stinted, but accepted in the fullest sense they will bear. And as it is certain that

God meant and ordained a use of the heavenly bodies in which they should "be for signs," and as we are here assured that what they have been arranged to signify is "the glory of God," there would seem to be ample scriptural warrant for believing that, by special divine order and appointment, the illustration of God's moral government, particularly as embraced in the story of sin, and redemption by Jesus Christ, is to be found in the stars, according to some primordial and sacred system of astronomy.

The roster of signs that would both precede and appear at His return, Jesus included: ". . . fearful sights and great signs shall there be from heaven" (Luke 21:11). "And there shall be signs in the sun, and in the moon, and in the stars . . ." (Luke 21:25).

We need to be aware as to the exact nature of these signs from heaven. The apostle John was shown an apocalyptic vision of the world during the last days of the Great Tribulation, and he wrote that because of the sun, ". . . men were scorched with great heat . . ."(Rev. 16:9). The prophet Isaiah wrote of this time: ". . . the light of the sun shall be sevenfold, as the light of seven days" (Isa. 30:26). Jesus said: "Immediately after the tribulation of those days shall the sun be darkened" (Matt. 24:29). The prophet Joel predicted that when the great and terrible day of the Lord would come, "the sun shall be turned into darkness..." (Joel 2:31).

For many years astronomers concluded that our sun

could maintain its present heat-energy output for at least five billion more years because its hydrogen supply was only about half exhausted. However, more recently, astronomers have reappraised this theory, and now believe that once a star (our sun is a medium-sized star) has expended half its hydrogen, it is in danger of experiencing a nova. Larger stars supernova (blow up), and smaller stars, like our own sun, nova—get brighter and hotter for seven to fourteen days, and then become darker. There are about thirty novas a year in the observable universe. Some astronomers now believe that increased sunspot activity is a sign that our own sun may be about to nova. The nova of our sun would most assuredly:

1. cause the sun to become unusually bright (as Isaiah prophesied),
2. become seven times hotter (as John prophesied),
3. and then become dark (as Joel and Jesus prophesied).

The Moon

Isaiah prophesied: ". . . the light of the moon shall be as the light of the sun . . ." (Isa. 30:26). Joel said of this time: "The sun shall be turned into darkness, and the moon into blood . . ." (Joel 2:31). Jesus said: "Shall the sun be darkened, and the moon shall not give her light . . ." (Matt. 24:29).

Inasmuch as the moon has no light of its own, and reflects only that light which it receives from the sun, the prophetic Word is in perfect harmony with science. It naturally follows that when the sun becomes seven times brighter, as Isaiah prophesied, its reflected light upon the earth will make the night as hot and as bright as an average day. Then, when the sun becomes dark, as Jesus said it must, the moon will naturally give off no light.

Even though some stars nova, they continue in a ringed configuration. Nevertheless, God the Creator will continue in control of the heavens and earth until his will and purpose is completed.

One theory as to why God created so many stars is to glorify His universal presence with habitations of those who would serve Him forever; not because they had to, but because they chose to. According to Revelation 12, one-third of the heavenly host chose not to serve and worship their Creator, but to follow Satan in rebellion. Thus, when the number of those who are saved through faith in His only begotten Son reaches the number of the angels who rebelled, then the Rapture will occur. While this is an interesting suggestion, there is no scripture to completely sustain it.

However, according to Ephesians 2:6, "And hath raised us up together, and made us sit together in heavenly places in Christ Jesus." Somewhere out there in the vast heavenly expanse there may be another star with its own solar system waiting just for me.

Numbers in Prophecy

Seven Days to Eternity

In 1776 Edward Gibbon finished his first volume of an encyclopedic set of historical research on the *Decline and Fall of the Roman Empire*. In his second volume of the six-volume set, chapter fifteen, Gibbon presented what the earliest church, even the apostles, had to say on the promised Kingdom age:

> The ancient and popular doctrine of the millennium was intimately connected with the second coming of Christ. As the works of the creation had been finished in six days, their duration, in their present state, according to a tradition which was attributed to the prophet Elijah, was fixed to six thousand years. By the same analogy it was inferred that this long period of labor and contention, which was now almost elapsed, would be succeeded by a joyful Sabbath of a thousand years; and that Christ, with the triumphant band of the saints, and the elect who had escaped death, or who had been miraculously revived, would reign upon earth till the time appointed for the last

and general resurrection. So pleasing was this hope to the mind of believers that the *New Jerusalem*, the seat of this blissful kingdom, was quickly adorned with all the gayest colors of the imagination. A felicity consisting only of pure and spiritual pleasure would have appeared too refined for its inhabitants, who were still supposed to possess their human nature and senses. A garden of Eden, with the amusements of the pastoral life, was no longer suited to the advanced state of society which prevailed under the Roman empire. A city was therefore erected of gold and precious stones, and a supernatural plenty of corn and wine was bestowed on the adjacent territory; in the free enjoyment of whose spontaneous productions the happy and benevolent people was never to be restrained by any jealous laws of exclusive property. The assurance of such a millennium was carefully inculcated by a succession of fathers from Justin Martyr and Irenaeus, who conversed with the immediate disciples of the apostles, down to Lactantius, who was preceptor to the son of Constantine. Though it might not be universally received, it appears to have been the reigning sentiment of the orthodox believers; and it seems so well adapted to the desires and apprehensions of mankind that it must have contributed in a very considerable degree to the progress of the Christian faith. But when the edifice of the Church was almost completed, the temporary support was laid aside. The doctrine of Christ's reign upon earth was at first treated as a profound allegory; was considered by degrees as a doubtful and useless opinion; and was at length rejected as the absurd invention of heresy and fanaticism. A mysterious prophecy, which still forms a part of the sacred canon, but which was thought to favor the exploded sentiment, has very narrowly escaped the proscription of the Church.

It is evident that the early Church fathers, dating from Peter, John, and the other apostles, believed and taught that the Millennium (Kingdom age) would come six thousand years after the creation of Adam. This was based on Psalm 90:4: "For a thousand years in thy sight are but as yesterday when it is past. . . ." Peter himself wrote in his Second Peter, 3:8: "But, beloved, be not ignorant of this one thing, that one day is with the Lord as a thousand years, and a thousand years as one day."

After Constantine and the establishment of the Roman Catholic Church, the church was going to bring in the Kingdom; therefore, the pre-millennial return of Jesus Christ was no longer needed nor taught. This doctrine was replaced with reformed or covenant eschatology, which stressed that the Church had inherited all the promises to Israel.

In Exodus 31:13–17, God through Moses impressed upon Israel that the people must keep the Sabbath, because the Sabbath was a "sign" of His covenant with that nation. A sign of what?

The writer of Hebrews, whom we believe to have

probably been Paul, wrote to the Messianic Church at Jerusalem that there was indeed coming a day of "rest," based upon the day that God rested, the seventh day (Hebrews 4:9–11). This day of rest, or "times of refreshing" referenced by Peter in Acts 3:19, is the Millennium when the Lord reigns on David's throne and all nations come bearing presents to Jerusalem (Rev. 20; Isa. 18:7).

If the Millennium, preceded by seven years of great tribulation, was to come in the year 6000 after creation, why isn't it here, as we are already into the seventh millennium by two years? There are some errors in our Roman calendar, but the signs of our time indicate that the coming of Jesus is near, even at the door (Matt. 24:33).

And even though we are not to know the exact date of our Lord's return, it seems evident that the apostles and early disciples were right on target.

Two Days to Christ's Return

In several prophetic passages, the number two is associated with the Second Advent, even in the Old Testament:

> For the children of Israel shall abide many days without a king, and without a prince, and without a sacrifice, and without an image, and without an ephod, and without teraphim: Afterward shall the children of Israel return, and seek the LORD their God, and David their king; and shall fear the LORD and his good-

ness in the latter days. . . . I will go and return to my place, till they [Israel] acknowledge their offence, and seek my face: in their affliction [tribulation] they will seek me early. Come, and let us return unto the LORD: for he hath torn, and he will heal us; he hath smitten, and he will bind us up. After TWO DAYS will he revive us: in the third day he will raise us up, and we shall live in his sight.

—Hosea 3:4–5; 5:15; 6:1–2

One of the primary things the prophets of Israel wanted to know in their communications with the Lord was when He would fulfill His covenant promises to the nation. In this representative story to Hosea, the Lord was not talking just about the Assyrian captivity or the Babylonian captivity. The Lord was telling Hosea how long it would be until Israel received their full blessing, even though it is doubtful that Hosea understood.

1. King David had already died when this prophecy was given. In some thirty verses in the New Testament, Jesus Christ is called the son of David; in at least ten verses His right to the throne of David is stated. Jesus Christ will sit on David's throne in the Millennium.

2. Jesus Christ did return to His place with the Father after His resurrection, because Israel rejected His right to the throne of David. When he returns, He will be given this throne.

3. Israel has indeed been scattered, torn and smitten

for two thousand years, the Diaspora. One-third of the Jews have returned.

4. It is obvious that the scattering of Israel would last more than two twenty-four hour days. It is obvious that the meaning is two thousand years—one day is as a thousand years with God.

5. Israel has not acknowledged Jesus Christ as Messiah, son of David, to this date; but in the Tribulation they will cry out for Him and acknowledge Him when he comes (Rev. 1:7; Zech. 12:10). Jesus said to Israel: ". . . Ye shall not see me henceforth, till ye shall say, Blessed is he that cometh in the name of the Lord" (Matt. 23:39).

6. In the third day, the third millennium A.D., the breach between God and Israel will be healed, and the nation will live again in His sight.

Two Pence Rent for a Thousand Years

We find another prophetic reference in the parable of the good Samaritan. A certain man, probably a Jew, was beset by robbers and grievously wounded. As he lay suffering in the road, a priest hurriedly passed him by without stopping, and likewise a Levite. A Samaritan, despised by both the priest and the Levite, stopped and cared for the victim's wounds. The Samaritan then took the victim to an inn: "And on the morrow when he departed, he took out two pence, and gave them to the host, and said to him, Take care of him; and whatsoever thou spendest more, when I come again, I will repay thee" (Luke 10:35).

Most Jewish priests and Levites lived in Jericho, a distance of about fifteen miles from Jerusalem. The road between passed through hills and ravines that robbers used for their bases. There was for many years a shepherd's inn on this road, but it probably was not the inn in the parable.

Most commentaries agree that in the time of Jesus Christ a pence was the cost of one day's stay at an inn; therefore, the Samaritan was paying for two days. The priests and Levites have been no help to Israel in the past two thousand years. The wounded and robbed man symbolized their condition. Only Jesus Christ will be able to help Israel when He will "come again." The two pence rent must be about all taken up.

Jesus said: "If I go away, I will come again."

The question is not if He is coming; but rather, when is He coming?

Guess Who Is Coming to Dinner

Every miracle that Jesus did was a fulfillment of an Old Testament prophecy regarding the Messiah. Jesus did indeed make the deaf to hear, the blind to see, the dumb to speak, and the lame man to leap as a deer. Jesus' miracles were just a promise to the world during the Millennium. But some of Jesus' miracles were previews in type of more definitive prophecies. Such is the case in the miracle of the feeding of about five thousand with five loaves of bread and two fish. It should also be noted that this particular miracle is recorded in all four gospels, which stresses its importance.

One of the gospels notes that the miracle occurred in the area of Bethsaida, which would be in the extreme northeast corner of the Sea of Galilee. It should be noted that there were five thousand men besides women and children, which would indicate there were somewhere between ten and twenty thousand present on the mountain. We also note there seems to be no separation between the men and women. Even today in Israel, men and women are separated in standard Jewish worship. In Christ, as Paul said, "there is neither male nor female."

Jesus said He had come only to the nation of Israel, and we read in Romans 15:8: "Now I say that Jesus Christ was a minister of the circumcision for the truth of God, to confirm the promises made unto the fathers."

Nevertheless, that Israel would reject Him was known by God, and through the atonement that He would accomplish, salvation by grace would be offered the Gentile world. Therefore, in some of Jesus' teachings and miracles we see truths for the Christian in type. In the miracle of feeding the thousands we note:

1. It was impossible to feed the thousands with what food was on hand at the time.
2. Jesus blessed five loaves of bread and they were sufficient to feed the multitude; because spiritually, He is the bread of Heaven (John 6:41,48).

3. As previously noticed in the chapter on number five, this is the number of grace. God's grace is more than sufficient to not only save five thousand, but more than five billion souls on earth today.

4. Jesus blessed two fish and they were sufficient to provide meat also for the multitude. Fish were the emblem of the early Christians. At Christ's birth the sun was passing into the constellation of Pisces, the fish, and now after two thousand years, typified by the two fish, the sun is passing into the constellation of Aquarius, the Water Bringer of the Latter Rain.

Four World Empires

God revealed to King Nebuchadnezzar of Babylon that from his time to the end of the Gentile age there would be four world empires:

> Thou, O king, sawest, and behold a great image. This great image, whose brightness was excellent, stood before thee; and the form thereof was terrible. This image's head was of fine gold, his breast and his arms of silver, his belly and his thighs of brass, His legs of iron, his feet part of iron and part of clay. Thou sawest till that a stone was cut out without hands, which smote the image upon his feet that were of iron and clay, and brake them to pieces.
>
> —Daniel 2:31–34

Daniel pointed to the king and announced, "Thou art this head of gold" (Dan. 2:38). The prophet then explained that his empire would fall to another and so on:

1. In 538 B.C. Babylon, the golden empire, fell to Medo-Persia (present-day Iran and Afghanistan).
2. Medo-Persia, the silver empire represented by the breast and arms on the image, fell to Alexander and the Grecian Empire in 333 B.C., the brass empire.
3. Alexander died in 320 B.C. His empire was split into four divisions, and subsequently overrun and absorbed into the Roman Empire in about 167 B.C.
4. The iron empire (Rome) represented in the legs of the image was to "break in pieces and bruise" (Dan. 2:40). In about A.D. 500, the Roman Empire broke into pieces, and the pieces created their own empires: German Empire, French Empire, Italian Empire, Netherlands Empire, Belgium Empire, Spanish Empire, English Empire, Danish Empire, etc. The major wars of the past fifteen hundred years were started between these pieces of the old Roman Empire, the latest being World War I and World War II.
5. According to Daniel 7:23, the fourth empire, even in a broken state, would, "devour the whole earth, and shall tread it down" (Dan. 7:23). During the Dark Ages and the Middle Ages, the Roman colonial empires of Europe had conquered and colonized all of Europe, all of Africa, all of South America, all of North America, Australia, most of Asia, and thou-

sands of the islands of the oceans and seas.

6. Going down the image, time is advanced, and in the toes of the image the iron chunks are broken into many small chunks. Toward the conclusion of World War II, the three surviving major powers were England, Russia, and the United States. President Roosevelt and Joseph Stalin forced Churchill of England to agree to a splitting up of the Roman colonial system.

7. Israel became a nation in 1948, and then nation after nation gained independence. The number of nations rose from seventy to over two hundred. As a sign of the end time, Jesus prophesied, "Behold the fig tree [Israel], and all the trees" (Luke 21:29).

8. According to Daniel 9, Revelation 17, and many other prophecies, in the extremity of the age, represented by the toes on the image, nations out of the original Roman Empire will reform the original Roman Empire and produce the Antichrist. This could be taking place in Europe today by the continued building up of the European Union from a commercial alliance to a political and military giant.

It was prophesied in 580 B.C. that there would be four world empires until the Messiah would come and establish His own Kingdom from Heaven that would never pass away.

Three World Leaders Die in One Month
In Zechariah 12 the prophet saw Israel as a nation again

in the end of the age, but beset with many enemies, Jerusalem a burdensome stone for all nations, and the army fighting against overwhelming odds. In the preceding chapter, chapter eleven, Zechariah in symbolic language depicts the conditions leading to the return of Israel in the last days.

Jesus said that He had come to the lost sheep of Israel (Matt. 15:24). Both disciples and the people of Israel are referred to as sheep needing a guiding shepherd. In Zechariah 11 the prophet references the last days in which the "flock of the slaughter" will be slain and those who kill them will say they are doing God's service, and even their own shepherds will not help them.

In verse eight of chapter eleven, Zechariah made a dire prophecy: "Three shepherds also I cut off in one month; and my soul lothed them, and their soul also abhorred me."

The persecution of the Jews in Germany before World War II began in 1935, and the literal Holocaust in which over six million Jews (including two million Jewish children) began in 1939. The two men most responsible for the Jewish Holocaust were Adolph Hitler and Benito Mussolini. Jews living in Germany were trapped, as most European nations, and the United States during the Franklin Roosevelt administration, refused to open immigration for Jewish refugees. The United States even refused to allow a ship carrying several thousand Jewish refugees to dock at any U.S. port. Most of the Jews on the ship later died in fulfillment of the prophecy.

Franklin D. Roosevelt died from a stroke on April 12, 1945.

Benito Mussolini was executed by insurgents on April 28, 1945.

Adolph Hitler committed suicide on April 30, 1945. "And I will bless them that bless thee, and curse him that curseth thee . . ."(Gen. 12:3).

All three died in one month!

153 Fish

Jesus Christ remained on earth for forty days after His resurrection (Acts 1:3), being seen by more than five hundred disciples at one time (1 Cor. 15:6). All that He did during these forty days is not recorded in the Bible. Forty is the number of testing or proving, and during this time the Lord did indeed prove to hundreds that He had risen from the grave. But one of the incidents in which Jesus appeared to the disciples was recorded by John.

In John 21:2 it is recorded that Peter, Thomas, Nathaniel, James, John, and two other disciples not named (seven in all), had been fishing all night in the Sea of Galilee and caught nothing. As the morning light appeared, they saw a man standing on the shore that they later perceived to be Jesus. Jesus instructed them to cast their nets on the right side of the ship. The net was pulled for two hundred cubits (about one hundred yards) and, after counting, they discovered they had caught one hundred fifty-three big fish. It would be a matter of fisherman's egotism that they counted the fish. I have never known a fisherman, including myself, who did not count the fish he caught, know the kind of fish, and how much they weighed.

However, the exact number of the fish has puzzled many scholars of the Bible. E. W. Bullinger observed: "This is a number which has taxed the ingenuity of some of the greatest of Bible students, and that from the earliest times."

Jerome interpreted the fish as being of all different kinds, thus the Gospel net to bring all races and nations into the Church. But there are not many kinds of fish in the Sea of Galilee, and at that time Jews would not have been proud of catfish. Even today, few Christian Jews will eat fish without scales. The dominant fish in the Sea of Galilee is the "peter-fish," and there is only one other lake in the world, as we have been told, that has this kind of fish. It is called a "peter-fish" because Jesus told Peter to catch a fish and look for a coin in its mouth to pay his tax. The mother peter-fish carries its young in its mouth until they get too big. After the minnows are gone, the mother fish looks for something to put in its mouth. The first time I baptized tour members in the Sea of Galilee, the peter-fish almost tore my toenails off. After that I always wore shoes. Jesus knew the mother peter-fish would have something in its mouth. In any event, this fish is of the bass family and good to eat, and kosher according to dietary laws.

However, Bullinger agonized over the puzzle of the

number one hundred fifty-three and finally came up with the possible solution that the sum of the value of the Hebrew letters in "Sons of God" amounts to one hundred fifty-three. John did share a new revelation with the Jewish believers in First John 3:2: "Beloved, now are we the sons of God. . . ."

But I personally doubt that this explanation fits the context of the story of the one hundred fifty-three fish. Ed Vallowe explained that one hundred fifty-three is the total of numbers one through seventeen; thus it is a soul-winning, fruitbearing number. The fact that no fish escaped the net signifies our security in Christ Jesus, so said Brother Vallowe. Makes sense, but there must be a more specific answer.

Several years ago as I was studying John 21, I analyzed every word and compared other scriptures that involved fishing with a net: ". . . the kingdom of heaven is like unto a net, that was cast into the sea, and gathered of every kind. . . . So shall it be at the end of the world" (Matt. 13:47,49).

Speaking of bringing Egypt to the judgments of the nations, Ezekiel prophesied: "Thus saith the Lord GOD; I will therefore spread out my net over thee . . ." (Ezek. 32:3).

There are at least twelve scriptures that prophetically speak of bringing the nations to judgment as with God catching fish or animals in a net. There are more than one hundred fifty-three nations in the world today, but we know from Matthew 25:31–46 that when Jesus

Christ comes to judge the nations with a rod of iron, the sheep nations will make it and the goat nations will not. Also, some of the nations today that have been created for a political or economical reason are not much bigger than my back yard, and I have a small back yard. My understanding of the one hundred fifty-three fish is that they represent one hundred fifty-three nations that will be under the kingdom rule of Jesus Christ when He returns.

But, we notice that there was another fish besides the one hundred fifty-three. This was the fish on the fire. This fish represents Israel during the Tribulation period:

> And it shall come to pass, that in all the land, saith the LORD, two parts therein shall be cut off and die; but the third shall be left therein. And I will bring the third part through the fire, and will refine them as silver is refined. . . . I will say, It is my people: and they shall say, the LORD is my God.
>
> —Zechariah 13:8–9

This alternate explanation of the one hundred fifty-three fish that I proposed several years ago has been introduced in some seminaries as an optional theory. In any event, the fish would not have been counted by Peter and John unless there was an important representation.

Seventy Weeks of Daniel

In the ninth chapter of Daniel we find Daniel reminding

God in prayer that the seventy years in Babylonian bondage, as prophesied by Jeremiah, had ended. Therefore, the prophet not only sought God's will for the Jews return to Israel, but he also asked when He would:

1. Finish the transgression of Israel against the Law.
2. Make an end of Israel's sins.
3. Make reconciliation for iniquity.
4. Seal up the vision and the prophecy.
5. Anoint the Most Holy.

According to Romans 11, and many other scriptures, we know that Jesus Christ came to fulfill the Law, offer Himself as an atonement for sin, and He would have reigned on David's throne had Israel accepted Him as the Messiah.

However, Daniel was told that all that he had prayed to God for would be granted at the end of seventy weeks. According to our weeks, that would be four hundred ninety days, or about one year and four months. It didn't happen, so we look for another explanation.

A Hebrew week could be seven days, seven months, seven years, etc. Jacob worked for Rachel one week (seven years) and got Leah, and then had to work another week (seven years) before he finally got her. And, as we have stated previously according to Scripture, one day with God can be a year or a thousand years. From the historical fulfilling of the first sixty-nine weeks of the prophecy, we can be certain that the four hundred ninety days were actually four hundred ninety years (Num. 14:34).

> Seventy weeks are determined upon thy people and upon thy holy city, to finish the transgression, and to make an end of sins, and to make reconciliation for iniquity, and to bring in everlasting righteousness, and to seal up the vision and prophecy, and to anoint the most Holy. Know therefore and understand, that from the going forth of the commandment to restore and to build Jerusalem unto the Messiah the Prince shall be seven weeks, and threescore and two weeks: the street shall be built again, and the wall, even in troublous times. And after threescore and two weeks shall Messiah be cut off, but not for himself: and the people of the prince that shall come shall destroy the city and the sanctuary; and the end thereof shall be with a flood, and unto the end of the war desolations are determined. And he shall confirm the covenant with many for one week: and in the midst of the week he shall cause the sacrifice and the oblation to cease, and for the overspreading of abominations he shall make it desolate, even until the consummation, and that determined shall be poured upon the desolate.
> —Daniel 9:24–27

The year that Daniel received the prophecy was 536 B.C. (some say 538 B.C.). Had the prophecy begun immediately, the Millennium would have occurred in 46 B.C.

But the clock on the four hundred ninety years was not to start until a decree was issued by Persia to rebuild Jerusalem. The rulers of Persia did issue several decrees permitting Jewish delegations to return to Israel to rebuild the Temple. The decree permitting the rebuilding of the walls and the city did not come until 445 B.C. (some say 444 B.C.). This decree is explained in the fourth chapter of Nehemiah.

7 weeks rebuilding the walls and streets   *49 years*
62 weeks later Messiah was to be cut off (die) <u>*434 years*</u>
                                                483 years

Forward on the calendar from 445 B.C. advances the date to A.D. 38. The seventy prophetic weeks would have been according to the Jewish calendar of three hundred sixty days a year instead of the three hundred sixty-five and a quarter days a year by our Roman calendar. Therefore, we have to deduct two thousand five hundred twenty-five and three-quarter days, or seven years and two months, bringing us back to A.D. 30.

Jesus would not have begun His messianic ministry until He reached the age of thirty years. However, there is a four-year error in the Roman calendar. Jesus did indeed minister to Israel for three and one-half years; cut off (crucified) in early April A.D. 30, four hundred eighty-three years after Artaxerxes of Persia issued a decree allowing the Jews to rebuild Jerusalem. No other Jew appeared at that time to contend for the throne of David;

therefore, Jesus had to be the Messiah, the very Son of God.

Dating back thirty-three and one-half years from the date of His crucifixion, Jesus would have had to be born at the time of the Feast of Tabernacles in late September, as we have always contended, and His conception by the virgin Mary at around December 25th, as we also have contended.

Sixty-nine of the seventy prophetic weeks has been fulfilled, but what about the one remaining week? When Jesus was crucified, the clock stopped. The clock will not start again until a man called the Antichrist signs a security treaty with Israel for one week, or seven years. After seven years of tribulation, a time Jesus said would be the most terrible period the world has ever seen before, Israel will believe that this Jesus whom was crucified is indeed their Messiah. The breach between God and Israel will be healed, and all that Daniel prayed for will be fulfilled:

> And there shall be upon every high mountain, and upon every high hill, rivers and streams of waters in the day of the great slaughter, when the towers fall. Moreover the light of the moon shall be as the light of the sun, and the light of the sun shall be sevenfold, as the light of seven days, in the day that the LORD bindeth up the breach of his people, and healeth the stroke of their wound.
>
> —Isaiah 30:25–26

What a Master Mathematician is our God to prophetically prove to the world by mathematics that Jesus is indeed our Christ Who was not cut off for Himself because He knew no sin. He died for your sins and my sins. Have you been born again by accepting (receiving) Him as your Savior and Lord?

Sixty-six and Counting

We are informed in Daniel 3 that King Nebuchadnezzar did not approve of Daniel's interpretation of his dream; especially the part about how his kingdom would fall to another kingdom. Daniel informed the king that his kingdom was represented in the head of gold on the image, so Nebuchadnezzar made the entire image out of gold to show God that his kingdom would last forever. The king was, in his own mind, greater than God; therefore, it is no wonder he made the image sixty cubits high and six cubits wide. The total of the two dimensions would be sixty-six. This is why Ed Vallowe in his explanation of the number sixty-six concluded that the number was associated with apostasy, or idol worship.

Michael Hoggard, in his book *By Divine Order*, takes the opposite view and identifies the number sixty-six with the worship of God, referencing the fact that our Bible has sixty-six books and the town of Bethel, which means "House of God," is found sixty-six times in the Bible. However, we are also reminded that it was at Bethel that Jeroboam set up an idol, the golden calf, for Israel to worship.

I think of the number sixty-six as the half-way house to 666 when a man will declare himself to be God. It has been said that if there were no God then man would either have to invent one or make himself God. The atheistic, evolutionary humanism of today is the religion of man worshipping himself. The sixty-six books of the Bible declare the true Creator to man, but when man does not accept the God of the sixty-six books of the Bible, he again turns to the image that Nebuchadnezzar erected on the plain of Durra.

144,000 Sealed Israelites

The chronology of Tribulation events appears to place a sealing by God of one hundred forty-four thousand Israelis before any of the apocalyptic judgments fall on the earth (Rev. 7:1–8).

Twelve is the number of government, 12,000 x 12,000 or 144,000, would certainly appear to be a Kingdom of God number, and we read that these are servants of God even before the sealing occurs. I have no idea the kind of seal each of these members of this group will have in their forehead, and at this point in time, I doubt if anyone else knows.

The number one hundred forty-four is found in only one other place in the Bible, and that is Revelation 21:17 where we read the walls of the New Jerusalem will be one hundred forty-four cubits high. We do find that the number of singers in the Temple choir was two hundred eighty-eight, or 2 x 144 (1 Chron. 25:7).

The tribes listed in Revelation 7 from which 12,000 are to come	Land portions for tribes in the Millennium (Ezek. 48)
Juda	Dan
Reuben	Asher
Gad	Nephtali
A'ser	Manasseh
Nephthalim	Ephraim
Manasses	Reuben
Simeon	Judah
Levi	Levi
	Benjamin
Issachar	Simeon
Zabulon	Issachar
Joseph	Zebulun
Benjamin	Gad

Joseph's two sons, Manasses and Ephraim, were given his lot in the land. The tribe of Ephraim went into idolatry more than any other tribe, possibly Dan excepted, and the tribe of Ephraim was mixed with other races during the Assyrian captivity. Most of the Samaritans came from Ephraim. The two golden calves were placed by Jeroboam in the city of Dan, and Bethel, which was in Ephraim's territory. Therefore, none are sealed from Dan, or seemingly, Ephraim. Instead of Ephraim, Joseph is mentioned, the father of Ephraim. This is somewhat puzzling, but it's God's problem, not mine.

Irenaeus in A.D. 180 forthrightly stated that the Antichrist would come from the tribe of Dan. Hippolytus in A.D. 200 wrote:

> "Dan is a lion's whelp" (Deut. 33:22). And in naming the tribe of Dan, he clearly declared the tribe from which the Antichrist is destined to spring. Just as Christ comes from the tribe of Judah, so the Antichrist is to come from the tribe of Dan.
> —Hippolytus (c. 200, W), 5.207

However, Dan and Ephraim will be given lots of land in the Millennium. As under the Law, the priests and Levites will live among the other tribes. But for purposes of witnessing during the Tribulation, twelve thousand will be sealed from Levi rather than from Dan.

Some point out that due to the dispersion of Israel into all nations during the Diaspora, it is impossible to know which Israelis today come from which tribe. Any Jew whose name is Cohen probably came from the Aaronic line; any Jew whose name is Levy, Levi, Levinson, etc., probably is a Levite. But even so, DNA testing now is proving that a Cohen really is from the priestly ancestral line. And, if microbiologists can tell which male fathered a baby, or which mummy came from which Egyptian Pharaoh, I suppose it would be possible to identify Israeli tribal ancestry. But as I have noted, God is much smarter than we are, and He will take care of the sealing.

And where are one hundred forty-four Jewish servants of God to be found immediately after the Rapture of the Church and the beginning of the Tribulation? Will they simply be religious Orthodox Jews or messianic Jews? Perhaps dramatic and startling events, like the Rapture of the Church, will turn many Israelis to Jesus Christ in the first days of the Tribulation.

Although not conclusive, the chronology of Revelation 7 would seem to indicate that the one hundred forty-four thousand will be in the world for three and one-half years, just as Jesus' ministry lasted for three and one-half years, and millions will be saved, but later killed by the Antichrist. During the first three and one-half years of the Tribulation, God will have given a witness before final destruction. He always does. Revelation 14 indicates the one hundred forty-four thousand will be taken out of the world at the middle of the Tribulation to allow the Antichrist to have complete control of the world.

The Biggest Number in the Bible

While there are no definitive numbers in the Bible as large as the national debt, there are some that doubtless stretched the imagination of the recorders of scriptures as they wrote. In Revelation 5:11 we read of ten thousand times ten thousand angels before the throne of God. This would be one hundred million angels, but John multiplied that number by thousands of thousands, increasing the angelic throng to an indefinite number in the billions or trillions.

There is a rather large definitive number in Revelation 9:16—two hundred thousand times one thousand, which would be two hundred million. This will be the size of the army from the East that will cross the Euphrates on the way to the Battle of Armageddon. Such an army at the time that John wrote the Revelation would have been impossible, but not today. In fact, Mao tse-Tung of China boasted that he could raise an army of two hundred million, the exact number mentioned by John. India today could also probably raise an army of two hundred million, but economics would probably prevent an Indian army of this size, at least at this time.

The fact that God would know two thousand years ago that in the future it would be mathematically possible to raise an army of two hundred million in Asia is in itself a verification of the coming Battle of Armageddon.

Mr. 666—You're the Man!

The apostle Paul wrote of the future world dictator who will rule over all nations during the coming Tribulation Period: ". . . that man of sin . . . the son of perdition; Who opposeth and exalteth himself above all that is called God, or that is worshipped; so that he as God sitteth in the temple of God, shewing himself that he is God" (2 Thess. 2:3–4).

While many ecclesiastics today refute the notion of a personal Antichrist, by reading the chapter on Antichrist in the *Dictionary of Early Christian Beliefs* by Bercot we find that Justin Martyr, Clement of Anesandria, Origen, Iranaeus, Hippolytus, Tertullian, and others of the earliest Christian pastors and theologians believed in the biblical, personal Antichrist who would:

1. Be Satan incarnate.
2. Reign over all nations in the seven-year Tribulation.
3. Kill the two witnesses of God.
4. Kill everyone who will not take his mark or number.
5. Kill everyone who will not worship him as God.
6. Desolate the world.
7. His name in the Hebrew, Roman or Greek number system would add to 666.
8. He will be destroyed by Jesus Christ at His Second Coming.

The early Church fathers may have not agreed entirely from which nation, race, or religion the Antichrist would come, but they agreed on the biblical warning about this coming man of sin. While many prominent political and religious personalities have had a name that added up to 666 in one of the language numerical structures, not one has had all the biblical qualifications—as yet.

We read of the Antichrist in Revelation 13:15–18 (thirteen is the number of sin and rebellion):

And he had power to give life unto the image of the beast, that the image of the beast should both speak, and cause that as many as would not worship the image of the beast should be killed. And he causeth all, both small and great, rich and poor, free and bond, to receive a mark in their right hand, or in their foreheads: And that no man might buy or sell, save he that had the mark, or the name of the beast, or the number of his name. Here is wisdom. Let him that hath understanding count the number of the beast: for it is the number of a man; and his number is Six hundred threescore and six.

Six is the number of man:
Man was created on the sixth day.
Man's time is measured by:
Sixty seconds in a minute (10 x 6).
Sixty minutes in an hour (10 x 6).
Twenty-four hours in a day (4 x 6).
Twelve months in a year (2 x 6).
Man has:
Six major members and parts.
Six quarts of blood.
Six senses.
Six hundred body muscles.
Normal height is six feet.
Average birth weight is six pounds.
When he dies he is buried six feet under.

The number 666 indicates a claim to human perfection, but it also indicates a trinity of evil: False Prophet, Antichrist, and Satan. Although we are told that no one will know the exact date of Christ's return, there is no indication that we cannot know that the Antichrist is in the world. Jesus told John that the number of his name would tell us who he is. Many Bible scholars believe that the Antichrist will appear out of the revived Roman Empire. The Roman alphabetical numbering system was:

I	—	1
V	—	5
X	—	10
L	—	50
C	—	100
D	—	<u>500</u>
		666

By ignoring all other letters in names, many have identified certain popes as having a name adding up to 666. Martin Luther said that a pope would be the Antichrist. Others have come up with 666 in the names of politicians and world personalities.

As far as the Mark of the Beast is concerned, modern technology makes it not only possible, but also desirable. Increasing world terrorism now demands universal and personal identification. Computer chips began to be placed in animals in the 1970s, along with the arrival of computer code markings on products. In March 2002, a family in Florida—as reported in *Time* magazine—volunteered to become the first computer chip implanted family, called the Chipsons.

With an increasing number of nations obtaining nuclear weapons, the world is looking for a solution to prevent human extermination. The Antichrist could promise a seemingly reasonable solution and be given the reins to world government by the United Nations. Regardless of how he comes to power, he will commit the Abomination of Desolation, referred to four times in Daniel, twice by Jesus, twice by Paul, and by John in Revelation 13. The "abomination" is his standing in the Temple Mount declaring himself to the world as God. The "desolation" of the nations of the world follows. Egypt will be desolated so that no living thing will live on the land for forty years, and Egypt will be in the middle of the other nations desolated (Ezek. 29).

Is the Antichrist in the world today? He could be. There is nothing unscriptural against putting a pencil to the numbers in his name.

One Thousand Missed Opportunities

The Hebrews did not have a number larger than one thousand. A million would be a thousand thousand, or one hundred million would be ten thousand times ten thousand, etc.

Adam and Eve were given stewardship over the Garden of Eden in which there were two trees about which God gave them special instructions. Had they eaten of the "tree of life" instead of the "tree of knowledge of good and evil," they would have lived forever in their earthly bodies. God had informed them that if they ate of the "tree of knowledge" they would die in that day. One day is with the Lord as a thousand years, as we have noted previously; Adam lived nine hundred thirty years. The oldest man in the Bible record was Methuselah, who lived nine hundred sixty-nine years before he died. No person has ever lived to be one thousand years old.

Because of sin becoming more prominent in the life of man, the life-span was gradually reduced, and today less than one percent of the human race live to be even one hundred years old. However, mankind will be given a second chance to break the one thousand-year age barrier. That will come after Jesus Christ returns to establish the Kingdom age, in which He will reign from Jerusalem and reverse the three curses that God placed on the environment. Some theologians and ecclesiastics scoff at the biblical teaching on the Millennium, but the thousand years of Jesus Christ on Earth is referenced six times in Revelation 20. If there is to be no Kingdom age for Israel, then at least one-third of the Old Testament needs to be deleted.

The scope of the thousand-year Kingdom age (Millennium) encompasses:

1. The establishing of political authority (Rev. 20:4). Jesus promised the twelve apostles they would sit upon thrones judging the twelve tribes of Israel (Matt. 19:28). The Tribulation martyrs will also reign with Jesus Christ.

2. Satan will be bound in the bottomless pit for the thousand years (Rev. 20:1–3).

3. The nations will be judged by the Mosaic Law, the Ten Commandments (Isa. 2:3; 42:4).

4. Capital punishment will be justly enforced (Isa. 65:20; Rev. 19:15).

5. Rulers of the nations will go to Jerusalem to worship the Lord (Ps. 2; Isa. 66:18–19; Zech. 14:16–20).

6. There will be no war for one thousand years; the nations will be at peace (Isa. 2:4).

7. In the Millennium the righteous will live in the flesh as long as the people before the flood (Isa. 65:22). But again, no one will live a thousand years. As the thousand years come to an end, Satan will be released to again tempt man. Man will have missed his second opportunity, and the age ends with judgment against all who failed the test.

The early Church fathers taught the biblical outline for a coming Kingdom age in which Jesus would reign in Jerusalem for a thousand years (*Dictionary of Early Christian Beliefs,* pp. 449–453). The Millennium is not a matter of opinion, but rather a matter of simply believing the Bible as God's Word.

Conclusion

Beyond the Millennium lies a New Heaven and a New Earth where time, distance, space, and numerics merge into eternity; when all of us who have been born again by faith in Jesus Christ will inherit heavenly places and boldly go where no man has gone before.

If in this humble attempt to address the glory, power, and majesty of God as the Master Mathematician we have in any way succeeded, then we thank Him for allowing us to touch even the farthest corner of His throne. And we pray that in some way we have brought the reader nearer to the Lord Jesus Christ in faith, knowledge, and fellowship (Phil. 3:7–9). If we have done this, regardless of our own imperfections, then we have succeeded in our intent.

*It is with infinite gratitude that I present the following
list of dear Christian friends, who through their
contributions have made this book possible.
May any good for the Kingdom of our Lord Jesus Christ
as a result of this book be credited to their heavenly account
for a just and eternal reward.*

—Noah W. Hutchings

Adams, Jackie
Adams, Lavonne
Affi, Leo
Aguilar, Capt. John & Sue Ellen
Alexander, Terry G. & Mernell
Allen, Mary L.
Anderson, Allan P.
Antonucci, Charmaine
Armstrong, James
Arnold, Rudy & Inga
Aubuchon, Donald & Debra
Augustine, Marion E.
Ayers, Lester
Ayres, John & Cathryn
Bacon, Jimmy
Bailey, Rodger & Dianne
Baisley, Mrs. Kathryn
Baldini, Mr. Demetrio, Jr.
Barnhart, Roy & Jackie
Bates, Donna & Lee
Bawulski, Fred
Baxiey, Mr. & Mrs. Olin
Beaman, Patrick

Beckwith, D.J.
Behnke, Roger & Dolores
Bell, Jean M.
Bennett, John
Benson, Vera Elizabeth
Bergman, Louis
Beyea, Jacqueline A.
Bidwell-Sooner, Sabrina
Bird, Sheri
Blanch, John S. & Lucy A.
Bloxham, James & Virginia
Bodanyi, Catherine Terese
Boehm, Christopher, L.
Bokum, Wayne J.
Boldor, Jean
Bonham, Jack L.
Bougsty, Larry
Bradford, Robert J.
Brady, Rachel
Brake, Roger, Jr.
Brandenburg, Glass
Brannon, Cindy
Brogden, Johnny

Bromberger, Eric

Brookshire, Pastor Wikie

Broscious, Lee R.

Brown, Fred J.

Brown, Gloria

Brown, Howard R.

Browning, Marilyn Ackerman

Bruce, Donna K.

Bruhn, Mr. & Mrs. B.H.

Bruhnke, Kyle & Doreen

Bryan, Mr. & Mrs. G.F.

Bryant, Timothy D.

Buchanan, John & Pat

Buck, Catherine A.

Buhrer, Patricia M.

Burness, Frances

Burns, Marilyn

Burns, Ralph W.

Cain, Cecil L.

Campbell, Maralou W.

Campbell, William & Karen

Capps, Ms. Martha N.

Carmical, Gene S.

Carnes, Bryan

Carper, Jewel

Carter, T.

Cepeda, Ms. Patricia Ann

Chambliss, Onil Bledsoe

Chaplin, Harold C., Jr.

Chaplin, Mr. & Mrs. William F.

Charles, Randy & Carma

Chatters, Hazel L.

Choate, Mrs. John D.

Cioffe, Mila

Claflin, Jim & Marcee

Clark, Lucille

Clark, Vonda

Clausen, Darryl A.

Cochran, Ruth

Coil, Wayne

Colao, Thomas F.

Callahan, Lloyd M.

Conner, Charles, J., Jr.

Cook, David

Cooper, Jan

Cooper, Jan

Cornett, Shane

Cotting, Mac & Jeanne

Cowden, Mr. & Mrs. John

Cox, Dean

Craddock, Louise H.

Craig, Charles & Marcia

Crandall, Marian P.

Cranford, Mr. & Mrs. James

Crick, Jerome, Sr.

Crockett, Terry

Crose, James & Janice

Cultivate Ministries

Cummings, Raymond

Curry, Bill & Ann

Cusack, Thomas D.

Dalton, Kenneth L.

Daluz, Joseph

Damisch, William M.

Davis, Dwayne

Davis, Rev. Frank A., III

Davis, Brent R.

Davis, Chuck

Decandia, Michael & Madeline

Dehart, Donald

Deleo, Jan

Delgado, Debbra

Demis, C.J.

Denileon, Richard

Denton, Mr. & Mrs. Clyde B.

DeOtis, Carol

DePledge, Kenneth

Derscheid, Ronald

Dettling, William

Detweiler, Tom

Detwiler, Jeff & Marianne

Devereaux, Bobbie Jones

DeVito, Debra Garsee

Dewey, Susàn (Loved of God)

Dickerson, James H.

Dickson, B.J.

Dirba, Ray & Margaret

Dodson, Sylvia R.

Doerr, Kenneth C.

Dollan, Ron

Dowe, Mr. & Mrs. Ken

Drinkert, David & Cheryl

Duff, Don

Duffett, Paul A.

Duffett, James R., PhD

Duffett, Henry P., Esq.

Duffy, Michael L.

Duncan, Joy

Duncan, Mr. & Mrs. W.E.

Dunlap, Douglas

Durant, Chas E.

Dye, Curtis & Maxine

Eades, Mr. & Mrs. Doug

Ebert, Doris M.

Edington, James C.

Elam, Israel R., Sr.

Ellis, Jim & Vail

Erks, Robert

Ermatinger, Mr. & Mrs. William

Eubank, Mrs. H.E.

Evans, Annie Jo

Ewing, Robert W.

Fahlen, Betty L.

Fareno, Thomas

Feinduer, Tim & Bette

Ferguson, Donald E.

Fida, Paulette

Filer, Mrs. Robert

Filingeri, Michael J.

Findlay, Bee

Fitzpatrick, Charles L.

Floyd, James S.

Floyd, Robert G.

Foery, Bill & Denise
Ford, Mrs. Mercedes B.
Ford, James
Forrest, Timothy
Forsman, Dan & Rhonda
Foulk, Lane & Debbie
Fountain, Mary
Frazier, Mrs. Virginia
Friend of God
Friske, Mrs. Harry "Pike"
Furber, Jim & Donna
Gail's Gift Shop
Gale, Mr. & Mrs. Dave
Garrison, Sally
Gartner, Fred
Gass, Hilda L.
Gaverluk, Alice M.
Gearhart, Lamoine O.
Geary, Allene
Gerlic, Richard H., MD
Gibson, Marie
Gill, Mark
Gillis, Richard A.
Gilroy, James V.
Gogolla, David
Gonsalves, Frances
Good, Mrs. Lynn
Goodenow, Craig M.
Goodson, Denise
Gorbin, William Emerson
Gordon, Peg

Gorton, Thomas G.
Gourmet Greens, Inc.
Granlund, Paul W.
Gray, Pastor Edwin E.
Green, Rollin G.
Green, Donna E.
Greve, Cal
Griffith, H. Gale
Griffitts-Wiser, Rebekah Earle
Grimes, Paul & Bonnie
Gross, Henry & Helen
Groves, Sheridon, MD
Guysinger, Ernest
Haas, Leonard
Hackney, Jack Deam
Hagen, Kenneth D.
Hale (Cox), Ann Loretta
Haley, Rev. Eric & Sally
Hall, Brian & Sherri
Halter, Ralph
Hamilton, John K.
Hammett, C.B.
Hancock, Mrs. Milton S.
Haney, Robert J. & Loretta M.
Hansen, Greg & Bonnie
Harbaugh, Martha L. Conner
Harper, Todd L.
Harrington, Eleanor E.
Harris, George P.
Hart, Mr. Richard
Hartman, Leonard

Hayward, Robert W.

Head, Wilma Louise

Hebel, Ronald

Heckman, Frederick S.

Heller, George Louis

Hendergart, David & Betty

Hennis, Vera Frances

Henricksen, M.J.

Henson, Lois M.

Herbst, Glenn G.

Heymann, A. Pauline

Hicks, Johann

Hill, Vaughn V., Sr. & Patricia

Hobbs, Gloria D.

Hobbs, Sandra

Hodge, Bill

Hoekman, Russel

Hoerner, Dick

Hoff, Peter

Hoipkemeier, Rev. Fred, MSO

Holt, Mrs. Ruth C.

Hoover, Dudley

Hopson, Sonja Lee

Horsey, Michael & Pamela

Horton, Elmer C.

House, Pernecia

Houston, Bonnie

Houston, Ruben

Howell, Mr. & Mrs. George E.

Howie, Lawrence B.

Huebner, Adele L.

Huggins, C.

Hunter, Grace K.

Hutchinson, Marilyn J.

Hylton, Ora P.

Ihlenburg, Jeanne

Ihlenfeldt, Rolf & Katherine

In His Service – The Goreckis

In memory of Robert Reynolds

Irick, Floyd B.

Jackson, John C.

Jackson, Mr. & Mrs. Thomas

Jackson, Geneva

Jackson, Vesta

Jenkins, Stan N.

Jesse, Kathi & Mike

Jetmore, Helen

Johnson, Dr. Pauline B.

Johnson, Richard & Virginia

Johnson, Charlotte

Johnston, Edwin E.

Jones, Mrs. Eliza P.

Jordan, Dr. & Mrs. Ron

Judd, Terry & JoAnn

Keck, Tom

Keller, Mel and Helen

Kelly, Mrs. Dorothy

Kelsey, Mr. & Mrs. Dale

Kiester, Ken & Joanne

Kilpatrick, Mrs. Chas W.

King, Bill & Shirley

King, Jerry C., Sr.

Kinsel, Gary L.

Kittle, Benjamin L.

Knight, Arthur & Deborah

Knight, Charles & Dana

Koester, James

Kohn, Tom & Cynthia

Kohr, Morgan

Komar, John

Korba, Andrew & Betty

Koster, Mr. & Mrs. David W.

Kostrzeba, Edward A., Jr.

Kraus, Connie M.

Krehbiel, Gary

Krueger, Edward A.

Kruse, Dorothy L.

Kujawa, Edwin S.

Kuykendall, Conni

Kuzma, A.H.

Lafoe, Flossie

Lang, George, Jr.

Laprade, Edward A.

LaPrath, Myron F.

Larson, Beverly

Lasewski, Kimberly

Latimer, Mr. & Mrs. W.

Laurito, Robert & Barbara

League, E.V. & Eileen

Leap, Edna M.

Leap, Marc

Lee, Donald Richard

Lee, Nancy

Lewis, Avalee

Lewis, Fredrick Earl

Lind, Mr. & Mrs. Robert B.

Lindemann, Ken & Violet

Lindsey, Homer M.

Lindstrom, David

Lindstrom, Mrs. Jessie

Linthicum, Mary E.

Lippy, J. Craig

Lisle, James D., PhD

Lithe, Mr. & Mrs. Virgil

Lockhart, Elva K.

Long, Mr. & Mrs. Robert D.

Ludwick, John

Luis, Mrs. Evelyn

Lussenden, Robert L.

Lyon, Esther

Madden, John & Jan

Madsen, Craig L.

Mahaffy, Hazel A.

Makua, Jan

Maldonado, Melva

Maley, Joseph G.

Mallery, Jan

Manly, Robert

Marburger, C. Orrie

Marks, Merritt

Marquardt, Mr. & Mrs. H.D.

Marshall, Dr. G. Ronald

Marshall, Albert Paul

Marshall, Mrs. FloAnn

Marten, Linda
Martin, Carl
Martin, Evertt Wayne
Martinez, Joe
Martz, Lee, Gwen & Family
Masoner, Mr. & Mrs. Paul
Mastromoro, John J.
Mathis, Betty Jean
Mattis, Mrs. Anne
May, Mr. & Mrs. William E.
May, Russell L. & Gale M.
McCabe, Jerry
McCarty, Mr. & Mrs. James E.
McClure, Mr. & Mrs. Bob
McCurdy, Ellen
McDuffie, Renae
McLean, Heidi
McLellon, Kenneth N.
McNeil, Peter
McNorton, Dr. Kathleen
McRoberts, Terry L.
Meyer, Frank O.
Milam, Rev. Emma
Miller, Stanley
Miller, Richard A.
Mills, Virginia
Mleczko, Kenneth R.
Moake, Agnes K.
Moerbe, Edwin C.
Moir, Edith, In Memory of
Hilda Moir

Monteith, Barbara & Stanley
Monteleone, Mr. & Mrs.
Nicholas
Montgomery, Mrs. Peggy
Montgomery, Jack
Moore, June & Victor
Moore, Larry & Dorcas
Morelli, Chet & Family
Morison, Richard W.
Morningstar, David
Morones, Gloria J.
Morris, Edward C.
Morris, Isabel
Moseley, Mrs. Ruth Grist
Mosley, Aaron
Moyer, Rex
Mullen, Jimmy & Phylis
Mullin, Wayne E.
Munro, Ethel T.
Murray, Harold
Musick, Edward C.
Musselman, William B.
Musulich, Mark
Nachtigal, Michael R.
Nahanee, Mr. & Mrs. Jack
Nealon, Joan M.
Negrete, John G.
Neises, Richard
Nelson, Harold R.
Nelson, Paul & Pamela
Nieto, Ray F.

Nix, Michael

Nixon, Kent & Kathy

Nortwick, R.H. Van

Noss, Nancy I.

O'Brien, Robert & Katherine

O'Dea, John

O'Toole, Paul W.

Oberholtzer, Diane

Oleary, Margaret L.

Olivieri, Mina

Oniga, Sharon

Onysko, David M.

Opper, Thurman J.

Orme, Ray Steele

Orvis, Wilda J.

Orzech, Joseph

Ostheimer, Paul J.

Ott, Helen & Richard

Otto, Richard F. & Yolanda I.

Palmer, Michael C.

Parker, Ed

Partin, Laverne

Patrick, Nora Gray

Paulgaard, P.B.

Payter, Ronald

Peck, Lorraine

Pelz, Janet

Pernecia House

Peters, Kenneth C.

Peterson, Charles & Sherryl

Peterson, Jeff

Phillips, Beau

Phillips, Scott & Tina

Pierce, Maureen H.

Pierson, Kathryn

Pisteh, George K.

Plank, Alistair

Polanskey, John, Jr.

Posey, John R.

Prahl, J.W.

Prather, D.

Pregano, Frank

Purnell, Greg & Rita

Quagliano, Anthony

Quinn, Jack G. & Rose L.

Raczelowski, Kathy & Stan

Raker, Lillian Albright

Reagan, David E. & Carol

Reaser, Kathryn J.

Reaves, Ms. Carolyn

Reeder, Joyce C.

Reel, Caroline

Reeves, Deloris G.

Relfe, Mary S.

Rettig, Chris

Rev. Michael L. Knetsch & Family

Rheinwald, Frances L.

(Daughter to Delores Kelly)

Rhoden, Donald

Richeson, Hugh A., Jr.

Ridderman, Eric

Riedell, Christopher M.

Rinck, Robert R.

Ring, Jean C.

Rivera, Manuel T.

Robacker, Mr. & Mrs. George & Lois

Roberson, Lee

Roberts, Angela

Roberts, Lonnie, Jr.

Roberts, Mr. Elliot C.

Rodriguez, Horacio H.

Rosendahl, Laurence & Dee

Rowden, Clifford E.

Ruby, Ralph

Sanders, Lisa Patrick

Santora, William

Saxon, J.

Scarfuto, Anthony

Scheulen, Ted

Schier, Larry

Schmidt, Stella L.

Schnell, Gloria J.

Schrag, Harold R.

Schroeder, Lowell & Betty

Schulte, Eugene & Beverly

Schultz, George

Schulz, Rick & Bonnie

Schwartz, William T.

Scott, Colleen

Scott, Norma L.

Scott Christian Ministries Pure Trust

Seltenreich, Mrs. Alberta

Servais, Geneva

Sery, Robert S.

Seymour, Bill

Shafer, Mrs. Sandy

Shaffer, Terry L.

Shlatz, Myron F.

Shuford, Miss Gail

Siegert, Kathy

Siemens, Irma M.

Skinner, Paul B.

Skold, Mr. & Mrs. Robert

Sloman, Betty

Smith, Clifford H.

Smith, Dr. Louise Kohl

Smith, James

Smith, W. Dean

Smull, J.T., D.S.C.

Snell, Raymond P., Jr.

Sole, Eugene & Cindy J.

Somers, Shirley

Sooner-Bidwell, Sabrina

Sorensen, Mr. & Mrs. Marvin

Souders, Beverly J.

Souders, John E., Jr.

Spalding, Vernon

Springfield, C.C.

Stackhouse, Frank

Stafford, Linda

Standeven, Mr. & Mrs. Robert

Starkey, Vicki

Stephens, Buzz

Sterling, Richard

Stoebner, Lloyd & Maxine

Stoops, David Lee

Street, J.P.

String, David & Linda

Stringer, Margaret

Stryker, J.G.

Stuart, Wanda

Stump, Mr. & Mrs. A.L.

Suess, Edmund F., PhD

Surrett, S.

Sutter, Ralph & Lillian

Swensen, Leota

Swenson, Richard W. & Phyllis

Switzer, Loren

Switzer, Lorraine

Szymanski, Diane

Taft, Ken & Bethel

Tan, Angel H.

Temple, William E. & Lorene V.

Terry, Mr.

The Robert Horton Family

Thieleman, William

Thomas, Dr. I.D.E.

Thomas, Evelyn Dolan

Tiegen, Mr. & Mrs. Don

Todd, Jonathan Michael

Tolles, Laura Lou

Tolson, Marjorie B.

Toretta, Bob

Tracy, Ella Jane

Trevino, Blanca Tripis

Trimmer, Kenneth, Jr.

Troesh, Carol

Trombly, John Victor

Trombly, Kirsten Noel

Trombly, Mark

Troy, Paul R.

Tsang, Alexander

Tubbs, Arnie M.

Tulock, Nick

Tuttle, Enid

Tyson, Jerry, Jody & Karyn

Underhill, Bill

Underhill, Dee

Underwood, Donald L.

Upton, Patrick C.

Vanderwerf, Richard

Varnell, Peggy

Vickery, Cecilia A.

Vogel, Bud & Cindy

Vorel, Donald E.

Voss, Larry D.

Walker, Bobby & Carolyn

Wallace, Mrs. Candice

Warren, Mrs. Doris

Weaver, Jack & Marjorie

Weaver, Mr. & Mrs. Jerald

Weaver, Mr. & Mrs. Richard O.

Webb, James & Marilyn

Webb, Louis F.

Weeks-Nyenkamp, Lucie

Weise, Volker & Iris

Weissburg, Doctor George

Wendt, Forrest & Gail

Whalen, Joyce

Wharton, Barbara E.

Wheat, Bill & Jackie

Wheeler, Lamar & Betty

Whitcomb, Dr. Walter & Juanetta

Whiteside, Penelope

Widmer, John P.

Wildermuth, Joyce E.

Wiley, Johnson H., Jr.

Willers, Suzanne E.

Williams, Howard

Wilson, Evangelist Christine

Windley, Walter H., Jr.

Winstead, Brian Norman

Witschey, Warren

Wolfe, David

Woodmansee, Mr. & Mrs. Wilfred

Woolsey, Steve

Worley, Arthur D., Jr. & Mary E.

Wozniak, Mrs. Barbie

Wright, Malcolm M.

Wright, R.M.

Wunderlich, Elge

Yerger, Ken & Renee

Young, Iona

Yukas, Terri

Zielke, Charles & Evelyn

Zimmerman, Gerald W.

About the Author

Dr. Noah W. Hutchings serves as president of Southwest Radio Church Ministries in Oklahoma City, Oklahoma. He has been with the ministry since April 1951, the same year he received Christ as Savior and Lord. He has written more than 100 books and booklets covering Bible commentary and prophetic topics. A member of the board of deacons of the Council Road Baptist Church in Bethany, Oklahoma, Dr. Hutchings is also a member of the University of Biblical Studies in Oklahoma City, and is a member of the Gideons organization.